EDGARDO FERNANDEZ CLIMENT

The AI-Driven Transformation of IT

A Leader's Guide to Navigating the Future of IT Infrastructure

Copyright © 2024 by Edgardo Fernandez Climent

All rights reserved. No part of this publication may be reproduced, stored or transmitted in any form or by any means, electronic, mechanical, photocopying, recording, scanning, or otherwise without written permission from the publisher. It is illegal to copy this book, post it to a website, or distribute it by any other means without permission.

Edgardo Fernandez Climent has no responsibility for the persistence or accuracy of URLs for external or third-party Internet Websites referred to in this publication and does not guarantee that any content on such Websites is, or will remain, accurate or appropriate.

Designations used by companies to distinguish their products are often claimed as trademarks. All brand names and product names used in this book and on its cover are trade names, service marks, trademarks and registered trademarks of their respective owners. The publishers and the book are not associated with any product or vendor mentioned in this book. None of the companies referenced within the book have endorsed the book.

First edition

This book was professionally typeset on Reedsy.
Find out more at reedsy.com

Contents

Preface   vii

I   Part 1: Setting the Stage

Chapter 1: The AI Revolution and Its Impact on IT   3
   Defining AI and Its Key Subfields   3
   The Convergence of AI, Big Data, and Cloud Computing   8
   How AI is Disrupting Traditional IT Paradigms   11
   Opportunities and Challenges for IT Leaders in the AI Era   15
   Summary and Key Points   18
Chapter 2: The Building Blocks of AI-Ready Infrastructure   20
   Hardware Considerations: GPUs, Specialized Processors, High-Performance Computing   20
   Software-Defined Infrastructure and Its Role in AI   23
   Data Storage and Management for AI Workloads   26
   Networking and Connectivity for AI   29
   Cloud vs. On-Premise Infrastructure for AI: Making the Right Choice   33
   Summary and Key Points   36

II Part 2: Transforming IT Operations

Chapter 3: From Reactive to Predictive: AI-Powered IT...   41
    The Limitations of Traditional IT Operations Management   41
    Introducing AIOps: Using AI for Proactive Monitoring, Anomaly Detection, and Automated Remediation   44
    Summary and Key Points   50
Chapter 4: Automating IT Infrastructure Management with AI   52
    Automating Resource Allocation and Scaling Based on Real-Time Demand   52
    AI-Powered Capacity Planning and Optimization   55
    Intelligent Ticketing and Automated Incident Response   58
    The Role of AI in IT Service Management (ITSM)   62
    Summary and Key Points   65
Chapter 5: Securing the AI-Powered Enterprise   68
    Unique Security Challenges Posed by AI Systems   68
    Protecting AI Models from Attacks   71
    Securing Data Pipelines for AI Training and Inference   74
    AI-Driven Threat Intelligence and Security Monitoring   77
    Summary and Key Points   80

III Part 3: Aligning IT with Business Transformation

Chapter 6: Data: The Lifeblood of AI and the Modern...   85

The Critical Importance of Data Quality, Governance, and Management for AI	85
Building a Data-Centric Infrastructure: Data Lakes, Data Warehouses, and Data Pipelines	88
Ensuring Data Security and Privacy in the Age of AI	91
Summary and Key Points	94
Chapter 7: AI-as-a-Service: Strategies for Adoption and...	97
Understanding the Different Types of AIaaS Offerings	97
Evaluating AIaaS Providers and Solutions	101
Integrating AIaaS into Existing IT Infrastructure and Workflows	105
Managing Costs and Ensuring ROI from AIaaS Investments	109
Summary and Key Points	112
Chapter 8: The Evolving Role of IT in the AI-Driven...	114
From Cost Center to Strategic Business Enabler	114
Fostering Collaboration between IT and Business Units	117
Developing New Skills and Competencies for the AI Era	120
Building a Culture of Innovation and Agility within IT	123
Summary and Key Points	127

IV Part 4: The Future of IT

Chapter 9: Emerging Trends Shaping the Future of IT...	131
Edge Computing and Its Implications for AI	131
Quantum Computing: The Next Frontier of IT Infrastructure?	135

The Rise of Serverless Computing and Its Impact on AI Workloads	139
Blockchain Technology and Its Potential Applications in IT	143
Summary and Key Points	146
Chapter 10: The Future of Work: How AI Will Reshape IT…	**149**
The Impact of AI on IT Job Roles and Responsibilities	149
The Skills Gap in AI and How to Address It	153
Upskilling and Reskilling the IT Workforce for the AI Era	157
The Importance of Continuous Learning and Professional Development	161
Summary and Key Points	165
Chapter 11: Building a Roadmap for AI-Driven IT…	**167**
Key Steps for Developing an AI Strategy for IT	167
Assessing Organizational Readiness for AI Adoption	171
Building a Business Case for AI Investments in IT	175
Measuring the Success of AI Initiatives in IT	179
Summary and Key Points	182
Conclusion	**185**
Summary of Key Takeaways	185
Call to Action	186
About the Author	188
Also by Edgardo Fernandez Climent	190

Preface

Artificial intelligence (AI) is transforming the world of IT at an unprecedented pace. As AI technologies continue to advance, they are revolutionizing the way organizations operate, creating new opportunities for growth, innovation, and efficiency. However, this transformation also presents significant challenges for IT leaders, who must navigate the complexities of AI-driven change while ensuring the continued stability and security of their organization's IT infrastructure.

"The AI-Driven Transformation of IT: A Leader's Guide to Navigating the Future of IT Infrastructure" is a comprehensive guide designed to help IT leaders, CIOs, CTOs, and business executives navigate the complex and rapidly evolving landscape of AI-driven IT.

This book provides a thorough understanding of the AI revolution and its impact on IT, as well as practical insights and strategies for transforming IT operations, aligning IT with business transformation, and preparing for the future of IT.

Through 11 chapters, we explore the key aspects of AI-driven IT transformation, from the building blocks of AI-ready infrastructure to the future of work and the skills required for success in the AI era. We examine the opportunities and challenges AI presents, the role of data in AI-driven decision-making, and the importance of security and governance in AI systems.

Our goal is to provide IT leaders with a clear understanding of the AI-driven transformation of IT and the skills and knowledge required to navigate this change successfully. We aim to empower readers to harness the power of AI to drive business innovation, improve efficiency, and create new opportunities for growth and success.

Whether you are an IT leader, a business executive, or simply interested in the future of IT, this book provides a comprehensive and accessible guide to the AI-driven transformation of IT. We hope that it will serve as a valuable resource for navigating the complex and rapidly evolving landscape of AI-driven IT and for building a successful and sustainable IT strategy for the future.

Key Takeaways from This Book

- Understand the AI revolution and its impact on IT
- Learn how to build AI-ready infrastructure and transform IT operations
- Discover how to align IT with business transformation and drive innovation
- Explore the future of IT and the skills required for success in the AI era
- Develop a comprehensive understanding of AI-driven IT transformation and its implications for IT leaders and organizations

I hope you find this book informative, insightful, and practical in helping you navigate the AI-driven transformation of IT.

I

Part 1: Setting the Stage

Chapter 1: The AI Revolution and Its Impact on IT

Defining AI and Its Key Subfields

As IT leaders, it's essential to understand the fundamental concepts and subfields of Artificial Intelligence (AI) to navigate the transformative journey of IT infrastructure. AI, in its broadest sense, refers to developing computer systems that can perform tasks that typically require human intelligence, such as learning, problem-solving, and decision-making. AI has been a buzzword for decades, but recent advancements have made it a critical component of modern IT strategies.

Defining AI

Artificial Intelligence is a multidisciplinary field that combines computer science, mathematics, and engineering to create intelligent machines. AI systems can perceive their environment, reason about the current state of affairs, and take action to achieve specific goals. AI encompasses various techniques, from simple rule-based systems to complex neural networks that mimic human cognition.

AI can be categorized into two primary types: **Narrow or Weak AI** and **General or Strong AI**.

1. Narrow or Weak AI: This type of AI is designed to perform a specific task, such as playing chess, recognizing faces, or translating languages. Narrow AI systems are trained on a particular dataset and incapable of general reasoning or decision-making outside their domain. They are the most common form of AI today and are often called "intelligent systems" or "smart systems."

2. General or Strong AI: This type of AI is hypothetical and refers to a system that can understand, learn, and apply knowledge across various tasks, similar to human intelligence. General AI would have the capacity for self-awareness, reasoning, and problem-solving, potentially more powerful and versatile than narrow AI. However, the development of general AI is still in its infancy and faces significant technical and philosophical challenges.

Key Subfields of AI

1. Machine Learning (ML): A subset of AI that focuses on developing algorithms and statistical models that enable machines to learn from data without being explicitly programmed. Machine learning is a crucial aspect of AI, as it allows systems to improve their performance on a task over time based on the data they receive.

- **Supervised Learning:** In this type of machine learning, the al-

gorithm is trained on labeled data, where the correct output is already known. The goal is to predict new, unseen data based on the patterns learned from the training data. For example, a supervised learning algorithm might be trained on a dataset of images labeled as either "cats" or "dogs" to learn how to classify new images.
- **Unsupervised Learning:** Here, the algorithm is trained on unlabeled data, and it must find patterns or relationships within the data on its own. Unsupervised learning is useful for discovering hidden structures or clusters in data, such as identifying customer segments based on their buying behavior.
- **Reinforcement Learning:** This type of learning involves an agent that interacts with an environment and receives rewards or penalties for its actions. The goal is to maximize the rewards by learning the optimal policy. Reinforcement learning is commonly used in applications like game playing, robotics, and autonomous vehicles.
- **Deep Learning (DL):** A subfield of machine learning that involves artificial neural networks inspired by the structure and function of the human brain. Deep learning models are particularly effective in image and speech recognition, natural language processing, and other applications that require processing complex patterns.
- ***Convolutional Neural Networks (CNNs):** Designed for image and signal processing, CNNs are a type of neural network that uses convolutional and pooling layers to extract features. They are widely used in applications like image classification, object detection, and image segmentation.
- ***Recurrent Neural Networks (RNNs):** Suitable for sequential data like speech, text, or time series data, RNNs use recurrent connections to maintain a hidden state that captures information from previous time steps. They are commonly used in language translation, speech recognition, and text summarization.
- ***Generative Adversarial Networks (GANs):** Consisting of a gener-

ator and a discriminator, GANs generate new data that resembles existing data, such as images or text. They have applications in data augmentation, style transfer, and image synthesis.

2. Natural Language Processing (NLP): Concerned with the interaction between computers and human language, NLP enables computers to understand, interpret, and generate human language. NLP is a key area of AI research, with applications in chatbots, language translation, and text analysis.

- **Tokenization:** The process of breaking down text into individual words or tokens, which is a fundamental step in NLP pipelines.
- **Named Entity Recognition (NER):** The task of identifying named entities in text, such as people, places, and organizations.
- **Sentiment Analysis:** The process of determining the sentiment or emotional tone behind a text, such as whether a customer review is positive or negative.

3. Robotics: The intersection of AI and robotics involves the development of autonomous systems that can perceive their environment and perform tasks that typically require human intelligence, such as assembly, navigation, and manipulation.

- **Computer Vision:** The field of study focused on enabling computers to interpret and understand visual information from the world. Computer vision is a critical robotics component, allowing robots to perceive and interact with their environment.
- **Motion Planning:** The process of determining a sequence of movements for a robot to perform a task, such as grasping an object

or navigating through a maze.

4. **Expert Systems:** These are computer programs that mimic the decision-making abilities of a human expert in a particular domain. Expert systems are based on knowledge representation and inference techniques, often used in applications like medical diagnosis and financial planning.

- **Knowledge Representation:** The process of encoding knowledge in a form that can be understood and used by a computer. Knowledge representation is a critical component of expert systems, as it allows the system to reason and make decisions based on the encoded knowledge.
- **Inference Engine:** The component of an expert system that applies the encoded knowledge to a specific problem or scenario, generating recommendations or solutions.

This detailed exploration of AI and its subfields provides a solid foundation for understanding the concepts and technologies driving the AI revolution in IT. In the next section, we'll delve deeper into the convergence of AI, big data, and cloud computing and how these technologies transform traditional IT paradigms.

The Convergence of AI, Big Data, and Cloud Computing

The AI revolution is deeply intertwined with the proliferation of big data and the rise of cloud computing. The exponential growth of data, combined with the need for scalable and cost-effective computing resources, has created a perfect storm for AI adoption. In this section, we'll explore the convergence of these technologies and how they are transforming the IT landscape.

The Rise of Big Data

"Big data" refers to the vast amounts of structured and unstructured data generated by various sources, including social media, sensors, IoT devices, and more. This data is characterized by its volume, variety, velocity, and veracity, making it challenging to process and analyze using traditional data processing tools. The sheer scale and complexity of big data have led to the development of new technologies and architectures designed to handle these massive datasets.

- **Volume:** The sheer amount of data being generated is staggering, with estimates suggesting that over 2.5 quintillion bytes of data are created every day.
- **Variety:** Big data comes in many forms, including structured data (e.g., relational databases), semi-structured data (e.g., XML files), and unstructured data (e.g., images, videos).
- **Velocity:** Data is generated incredibly, with real-time data streams from sources like social media, sensors, and IoT devices.

- **Veracity:** The accuracy and reliability of the data are critical, as poor data quality can lead to inaccurate insights and decisions.

The Role of Cloud Computing

Cloud computing has emerged as a key enabler of AI adoption, providing scalability, flexibility, and cost savings for AI workloads. Cloud infrastructure offers a range of benefits, including:

- **Scalability:** Cloud resources can be quickly scaled up or down to meet changing demands, making it an ideal platform for AI workloads that require massive computational resources.
- **Flexibility:** Cloud providers offer a range of services, from infrastructure as a service (IaaS) to platform as a service (PaaS) and software as a service (SaaS), allowing organizations to choose the level of control and management they require.
- **Cost Savings:** Cloud computing eliminates the need for upfront capital expenditures on hardware and reduces operational expenses, making it a cost-effective option for AI initiatives.

The Intersection of AI, Big Data, and Cloud Computing

The convergence of AI, big data, and cloud computing is driving the AI revolution in IT. Here's how these technologies intersect:

- **Data Ingestion and Processing:** Cloud-based data ingestion and processing platforms, such as Apache NiFi and Apache Spark, enable the rapid ingestion and processing of large datasets. These platforms are designed to handle the volume, variety, and velocity of big data, making them ideal for AI applications.
- **AI Model Training and Deployment:** Cloud providers offer AI-specific services, such as Google Cloud AI Platform, Amazon SageMaker, and Microsoft Azure Machine Learning, that simplify the training and deployment of AI models. These services provide pre-built algorithms, automated model training, and deployment options, making it easier to integrate AI into existing IT infrastructure.
- **Data Storage and Management:** Cloud-based data storage solutions, such as object storage and data lakes, provide a scalable and cost-effective way to store and manage large datasets. These solutions are designed to handle the volume and variety of big data, making them ideal for AI applications.
- **Real-Time Analytics and Insights:** Cloud-based analytics platforms, such as Google Cloud Bigtable and Amazon Redshift, enable real-time analytics and insights from big data. These platforms are designed to handle the velocity of big data, providing organizations with timely insights to inform business decisions.

The Impact on IT Infrastructure

The convergence of AI, big data, and cloud computing is transforming traditional IT infrastructure in several ways:

- **Scalability and Flexibility:** Cloud computing has made it possible

to scale IT infrastructure up or down as needed, providing the flexibility to adapt to changing business requirements.
- **Automation and Orchestration:** The use of AI and automation tools has enabled the automation of many IT tasks, freeing up resources for more strategic activities.
- **New Skills and Competencies:** Adopting AI, big data, and cloud computing requires new skills and competencies, such as data science, machine learning engineering, and cloud architecture.
- **Security and Governance:** The increased use of cloud and AI technologies has introduced new security and governance challenges, such as data privacy, model explainability, and AI-specific security threats.

The convergence of AI, big data, and cloud computing is a powerful force driving the transformation of IT infrastructure. As IT leaders, it's essential to understand the interplay between these technologies and how they are reshaping the IT landscape. By embracing these technologies, organizations can unlock new insights, improve operational efficiency, and drive business innovation.

How AI is Disrupting Traditional IT Paradigms

The AI revolution is not just a technological advancement; it's a transformative force that's reshaping the very fabric of IT operations. As AI continues to permeate every aspect of IT, traditional paradigms are being disrupted, and new opportunities and challenges are emerging. In this section, we'll explore how AI disrupts traditional IT paradigms and the implications for IT leaders.

Automation and Augmentation

AI automates many routine and repetitive tasks, freeing IT resources for more strategic activities. This automation is not limited to simple tasks; AI is also augmenting human capabilities, enabling IT professionals to focus on higher-value tasks that require creativity, empathy, and complex decision-making.

- **IT Service Management (ITSM):** AI-powered ITSM tools are automating incident management, problem management, and change management, reducing the mean time to resolve (MTTR) and increasing the mean time between failures (MTBF).
- **Network Management:** AI-driven network management systems predict and prevent network outages, reduce downtime, and improve network reliability.
- **Cybersecurity:** AI-powered security tools detect and respond to threats in real-time, reducing the risk of security breaches and improving incident response times.

Predictive Maintenance and Proactive Operations

AI enables predictive maintenance and proactive operations, allowing IT teams to anticipate and prevent issues before they occur. This shift from reactive to proactive operations transforms how IT teams work.

- **Predictive Analytics:** AI-powered predictive analytics identify potential issues before they occur, enabling IT teams to take

proactive measures to prevent downtime and improve system reliability.
- **Anomaly Detection:** AI-driven anomaly detection systems identify unusual patterns in system behavior, enabling IT teams to take swift action to prevent issues from escalating.
- **Root Cause Analysis:** AI-powered root cause analysis tools are identifying the underlying causes of issues, enabling IT teams to address the root cause rather than just the symptoms.

Enhanced Customer Experience

AI is revolutionizing the customer experience by providing personalized and efficient support. Chatbots, virtual assistants, and AI-powered help desks are becoming the norm, enabling organizations to offer 24/7 support and improving customer satisfaction.

- **Chatbots and Virtual Assistants:** AI-powered chatbots and virtual assistants are providing personalized support, answering common queries, and routing complex issues to human support agents.
- **Sentiment Analysis:** AI-powered sentiment analysis tools analyze customer feedback, enabling organizations to identify areas for improvement and measure customer satisfaction.
- **Personalization:** AI-powered personalization engines tailor the customer experience to individual preferences, improving engagement and loyalty.

New Skills and Competencies

Adopting AI introduces new skills and competencies that IT professionals must possess to remain relevant. IT leaders must invest in upskilling and reskilling their teams to ensure they can work effectively with AI technologies.

- **Data Science and Machine Learning:** IT professionals must understand the fundamentals of data science and machine learning to develop and deploy AI models.
- **Cloud and Infrastructure:** IT professionals must understand cloud infrastructure and how to deploy and manage AI workloads in the cloud.
- **Automation and Orchestration:** IT professionals must understand automation and orchestration tools to integrate AI into IT workflows.

Ethical Considerations

The increasing use of AI raises ethical considerations that IT leaders must address. These include bias in AI models, data privacy, and the potential impact of AI on employment.

- **Bias in AI Models:** AI models can perpetuate biases in the training data, leading to unfair outcomes. IT leaders must ensure that AI models are trained on diverse datasets and are regularly audited for bias.

- **Data Privacy:** AI models require access to vast data, raising concerns about privacy and security. IT leaders must ensure data is properly secured and privacy regulations are followed.
- **Job Displacement:** The automation of tasks by AI raises concerns about job displacement. IT leaders must ensure that the benefits of AI are shared fairly and that workers are upskilled to work alongside AI systems.

The AI revolution disrupts traditional IT paradigms, introducing new opportunities and challenges. IT leaders must understand these disruptions and adapt their strategies to leverage the benefits of AI while mitigating its risks. By embracing AI, organizations can improve operational efficiency, enhance customer experience, and drive business innovation. However, it's crucial to address the ethical considerations and ensure that AI is used responsibly and for the greater good.

Opportunities and Challenges for IT Leaders in the AI Era

As AI continues to transform the IT landscape, leaders face both opportunities and challenges. In this section, we'll delve into the key opportunities and challenges that IT leaders must navigate to leverage AI in their organizations successfully.

Opportunities

- **Increased Efficiency:** AI can automate routine and repetitive tasks, freeing IT resources for more strategic activities. This increased efficiency can lead to cost savings, improved productivity, and enhanced customer satisfaction.
- **Improved Decision-Making:** AI-driven insights can inform business decisions, leading to better outcomes. By leveraging AI, IT leaders can make data-driven decisions, reducing the risk of human bias and error.
- **Enhanced Customer Experience:** AI-powered systems can provide personalized and efficient support, improving customer satisfaction and loyalty. Chatbots, virtual assistants, and AI-powered help desks are becoming the norm, enabling organizations to offer 24/7 support.
- **Competitive Advantage:** Organizations that successfully leverage AI can gain a competitive advantage over their peers. AI can enable businesses to innovate faster, respond quickly to changing market conditions, and create new revenue streams.
- **New Business Models:** AI enables new business models, such as AI-as-a-Service, to generate new revenue streams and create new growth opportunities.

Challenges

- **Skills Gap:** Adopting AI requires new skills and competencies, such as data science, machine learning engineering, and cloud architecture. IT leaders must invest in upskilling and reskilling their teams to ensure they can work effectively with AI technologies.

- **Data Quality:** AI models are only as good as the data they're trained on. IT leaders must ensure that data is accurate, complete, and relevant to achieve reliable insights and decisions.
- **Ethical Considerations:** The increasing use of AI raises ethical considerations, such as bias in AI models, data privacy, and the potential impact of AI on employment. IT leaders must ensure that AI is used responsibly and for the greater good.
- **Change Management:** Adopting AI requires significant changes to existing IT workflows and processes. IT leaders must manage this change effectively to minimize disruption and ensure a smooth transition.
- **Cybersecurity:** AI introduces new cybersecurity risks, such as AI-powered attacks and data breaches. IT leaders must ensure their organizations are prepared to address these risks and protect their systems and data.

Key Takeaways

- AI offers significant opportunities for IT leaders, including increased efficiency, improved decision-making, enhanced customer experience, competitive advantage, and new business models.
- However, AI also presents challenges, such as the skills gap, data quality, ethical considerations, change management, and cybersecurity risks.
- IT leaders must navigate these opportunities and challenges to leverage AI successfully.

By understanding these opportunities and challenges, IT leaders can develop strategies to harness the power of AI and drive business success. In the next chapter, we'll explore the building blocks of AI-ready infrastructure, including hardware, software, and networking considerations.

Summary and Key Points

In this chapter, we've set the stage for the AI-driven transformation of IT by defining AI and its key subfields, exploring the convergence of AI, big data, and cloud computing, and discussing how AI is disrupting traditional IT paradigms. We've also examined the opportunities and challenges that AI presents for IT leaders.

Summary

The AI revolution is transforming the IT landscape, offering significant opportunities for increased efficiency, improved decision-making, enhanced customer experience, competitive advantage, and new business models. However, AI also presents challenges, such as the skills gap, data quality, ethical considerations, change management, and cybersecurity risks. To successfully leverage AI, IT leaders must understand these opportunities and challenges and develop strategies to harness the power of AI.

CHAPTER 1: THE AI REVOLUTION AND ITS IMPACT ON IT

Key Points

1. AI is a broad field encompassing machine learning, deep learning, NLP, robotics, and expert systems.

2. The convergence of AI, big data, and cloud computing drives the AI revolution in IT, enabling real-time analytics, automated model training, and scalable data storage.

3. AI disrupts traditional IT paradigms through automation, predictive maintenance, enhanced customer experience, and cybersecurity.

4. IT leaders must navigate the opportunities and challenges of AI, including increased efficiency, improved decision-making, enhanced customer experience, competitive advantage, and new business models, as well as the skills gap, data quality, ethical considerations, change management, and cybersecurity risks.

In the next chapter, we'll delve into the building blocks of AI-ready infrastructure, exploring the hardware, software, and networking considerations necessary for supporting AI workloads. This will provide a solid foundation for understanding the technical requirements of AI adoption and how to build an infrastructure that can support the demands of AI applications.

Chapter 2: The Building Blocks of AI-Ready Infrastructure

Hardware Considerations: GPUs, Specialized Processors, High-Performance Computing

As AI workloads continue to grow in complexity and scale, traditional hardware infrastructure is often insufficient to meet the demands of these applications. In this section, we'll explore the hardware considerations necessary for building an AI-ready infrastructure, including GPUs, specialized processors, and high-performance computing.

Graphics Processing Units (GPUs)

GPUs have emerged as a critical component of AI infrastructure due to their ability to handle massive parallel processing, which is essential for deep learning and other AI workloads. GPUs offer several advantages over traditional central processing units (CPUs):

- **Parallel Processing:** GPUs are designed to handle thousands of

threads simultaneously, making them much faster than CPUs for parallelizable workloads like deep learning.
- **Memory Bandwidth:** GPUs have higher memory bandwidth than CPUs, enabling faster data transfer and processing.
- **Power Efficiency:** GPUs are more power-efficient than CPUs, reducing the overall energy consumption of AI workloads.

Specialized Processors

Specialized processors, such as TPUs (Tensor Processing Units) and ASICs (Application-Specific Integrated Circuits), are designed specifically for AI workloads. These processors offer significant performance and power efficiency improvements over traditional CPUs and GPUs:

- **TPUs:** Developed by Google, TPUs are custom-built ASICs designed specifically for machine learning and deep learning workloads. They offer significant performance improvements over GPUs for these specific workloads.
- **ASICs:** ASICs are custom-designed processors for specific tasks, such as AI acceleration. They offer the highest performance and power efficiency for their target workloads.

High-Performance Computing (HPC)

HPC is a critical component of AI infrastructure, enabling the processing of massive datasets and complex AI models. HPC environments typically consist of the following:

- **Clusters:** Clusters of servers, often with GPUs or specialized processors, that work together to process large datasets.
- **Distributed Computing:** Distributed computing frameworks, such as Hadoop and Spark, enable the processing of large datasets across multiple nodes.
- **Storage:** High-performance storage solutions, such as parallel file systems and object storage, are necessary to handle the massive amounts of data generated by AI workloads.

Key Considerations for AI-Ready Hardware

When selecting hardware for AI workloads, several key considerations must be taken into account:

- **Scalability:** The ability to scale hardware resources up or down as needed is critical for AI workloads, which can vary significantly in computational requirements.
- **Interconnects:** High-speed interconnects, such as InfiniBand and NVLink, are necessary to ensure fast data transfer between nodes in a cluster.
- **Cooling and Power:** AI workloads can generate significant heat and

consume large amounts of power. Cooling and power management are critical considerations for AI-ready hardware.
- **Memory and Storage:** Adequate memory and storage are essential for handling large datasets and complex AI models.

The hardware considerations for AI-ready infrastructure are critical to ensuring the successful deployment and operation of AI workloads. By understanding the role of GPUs, specialized processors, and high-performance computing, IT leaders can build an infrastructure that meets the demands of AI applications. In the next section, we'll explore software-defined infrastructure and its role in AI.

Software-Defined Infrastructure and Its Role in AI

Software-defined infrastructure (SDI) is a critical component of AI-ready infrastructure, enabling the automation, orchestration, and management of AI workloads. In this section, we'll explore the role of SDI in AI and how it supports the deployment and operation of AI applications.

What is Software-Defined Infrastructure?

SDI is an approach to IT infrastructure that uses software to manage and control the infrastructure rather than relying on traditional hardware-defined infrastructure. SDI enables the virtualization of compute, storage, and networking resources, making it easier to manage and scale infrastructure to meet changing business needs.

Key Components of SDI

- **Software-Defined Compute (SDC):** SDC enables the virtualization of compute resources, allowing for the creation of virtual machines, containers, and serverless functions.
- **Software-Defined Storage (SDS):** SDS enables the virtualization of storage resources, providing a single, unified view of storage across the infrastructure.
- **Software-Defined Networking (SDN):** SDN enables the virtualization of networking resources, allowing for the creation of virtual networks and the automation of network configuration.

The Role of SDI in AI

SDI plays a critical role in supporting AI workloads by:

- **Simplifying Infrastructure Management:** SDI simplifies the management of AI infrastructure, enabling IT teams to focus on higher-value tasks.
- **Enabling Scalability:** SDI enables the rapid scaling of infrastructure resources to meet the changing demands of AI workloads.
- **Improving Resource Utilization:** SDI improves resource utilization by enabling the sharing of resources across multiple workloads.
- **Enhancing Security:** SDI improves security by providing a single, unified view of the infrastructure and enabling the automation of

CHAPTER 2: THE BUILDING BLOCKS OF AI-READY INFRASTRUCTURE

security policies.

SDI and AI Workloads

SDI is particularly well-suited to support AI workloads due to their unique requirements:

- **Elasticity:** AI workloads often require rapid scaling up or down to meet changing computational demands. SDI enables this elasticity, ensuring that resources are available when needed.
- **Automation:** AI workloads often require automation to manage the complexity of the workflow. SDI enables the automation of infrastructure management, freeing up IT resources for more strategic activities.
- **Flexibility:** AI workloads often require flexibility in terms of infrastructure configuration. SDI enables this flexibility, allowing for the rapid reconfiguration of infrastructure to meet changing business needs.

Key SDI Technologies for AI

Several SDI technologies are critical for supporting AI workloads:

- **Kubernetes:** Kubernetes is an open-source container orchestration system that enables the automation of container deployment,

scaling, and management.
- **OpenStack:** OpenStack is an open-source cloud computing platform that enables the creation of a private cloud infrastructure.
- **VMware vSphere:** VMware vSphere is a virtualization platform that enables the creation of a virtualized infrastructure.

Software-defined infrastructure is a critical component of AI-ready infrastructure, enabling the automation, orchestration, and management of AI workloads. By understanding the role of SDI in AI, IT leaders can build an infrastructure that meets the unique demands of AI applications. In the next section, we'll explore data storage and management for AI workloads.

Data Storage and Management for AI Workloads

Data storage and management are critical components of AI-ready infrastructure, as AI workloads rely heavily on large datasets for training and inference. In this section, we'll explore the data storage and management considerations necessary for supporting AI workloads.

Data Storage Requirements for AI

AI workloads have unique data storage requirements, including:

- **Scalability:** AI datasets can be massive, requiring scalable storage solutions to handle large amounts of data.

- **Performance:** AI workloads require high-performance storage for fast data access and processing.
- **Data Variety:** AI datasets can include structured, semi-structured, and unstructured data, requiring storage solutions that can handle diverse data formats.

Data Storage Options for AI

Several data storage options are suitable for AI workloads, including:

- **Object Storage:** Object storage solutions, such as Amazon S3 and Ceph, are designed for storing large amounts of unstructured data and are often used for AI datasets.
- **File Systems:** File systems, such as HDFS and NFS, are designed for storing structured and semi-structured data and are often used for AI datasets.
- **Databases:** Databases, such as relational databases and NoSQL databases, are designed for storing structured data and are often used for AI datasets.

Data Management for AI

Effective data management is critical for AI workloads, including:

- **Data Ingestion:** Data ingestion involves collecting and transporting

data from various sources to a central location for processing.
- **Data Processing:** Data processing involves transforming and preparing data for AI model training and inference.
- **Data Versioning:** Data versioning involves the management of different versions of datasets and AI models to ensure reproducibility and auditability.

Data Governance for AI

Data governance is critical for AI workloads, including:

- **Data Quality:** Ensuring the quality of AI datasets is essential to ensure the accuracy and reliability of AI models.
- **Data Security:** Ensuring the security of AI datasets is critical to prevent unauthorized access and ensure compliance with regulations.
- **Data Lineage:** Data lineage involves the tracking of data provenance and movement through the AI workflow to ensure transparency and auditability.

Key Considerations for AI Data Storage and Management

When selecting data storage and management solutions for AI workloads, several key considerations must be taken into account:

- **Scalability:** The ability to scale storage resources up or down as

needed is critical for AI workloads.
- **Performance:** High-performance storage is necessary to ensure fast data access and processing.
- **Data Variety:** Storage solutions must be able to handle diverse data formats and structures.
- **Security:** Data security is critical to prevent unauthorized access and ensure regulation compliance.
- **Governance:** Effective data governance is necessary to ensure data quality, security, and lineage.

Data storage and management are critical components of AI-ready infrastructure, enabling the efficient and effective processing of large datasets. By understanding the data storage and management considerations for AI workloads, IT leaders can build an infrastructure that meets the unique demands of AI applications. In the next section, we'll explore networking and connectivity for AI workloads.

Networking and Connectivity for AI

Networking and connectivity are critical components of AI-ready infrastructure, as AI workloads rely heavily on high-bandwidth, low-latency connections to ensure fast data transfer and processing. In this section, we'll explore the networking and connectivity considerations necessary for supporting AI workloads.

Networking Requirements for AI

AI workloads have unique networking requirements, including:

- **High Bandwidth:** AI workloads require high-bandwidth connections to ensure fast data transfer between nodes and to/from storage.
- **Low Latency:** AI workloads require low-latency connections to ensure fast processing and real-time inference.
- **Reliability:** AI workloads require reliable connections to ensure continuous operation and minimize downtime.

Networking Technologies for AI

Several networking technologies are suitable for AI workloads, including:

- **Ethernet:** Ethernet is a widely used networking technology that provides high-bandwidth connections.
- **InfiniBand:** InfiniBand is a high-speed networking technology that provides low-latency connections.
- **Fibre Channel:** Fibre Channel is a high-speed networking technology that provides high-bandwidth connections for storage area networks (SANs).

Networking Architectures for AI

Several networking architectures are suitable for AI workloads, including:

- **Leaf-Spine Architecture:** Leaf-spine architecture is a common data center architecture that provides high-bandwidth connections and low latency.
- **Clos Network Architecture:** Clos network architecture is a scalable and flexible architecture that provides high-bandwidth connections and low latency.
- **Spine-Leaf Architecture:** Spine-leaf architecture is a variant of leaf-spine architecture that provides high-bandwidth connections and low latency.

Connectivity Options for AI

Several connectivity options are suitable for AI workloads, including:

- **10GbE:** 10GbE (10 Gigabit Ethernet) is a high-bandwidth connectivity option that provides fast data transfer.
- **25GbE:** 25GbE (25 Gigabit Ethernet) is a high-bandwidth connectivity option that provides fast data transfer.
- **40GbE:** 40GbE (40 Gigabit Ethernet) is a high-bandwidth connectivity option that provides fast data transfer.
- **100GbE:** 100GbE (100 Gigabit Ethernet) is a high-bandwidth connectivity option that provides fast data transfer.

Key Considerations for AI Networking and Connectivity

When selecting networking and connectivity solutions for AI workloads, several key considerations must be taken into account:

- **Bandwidth:** The bandwidth requirements of AI workloads must be carefully considered to ensure fast data transfer.
- **Latency:** The latency requirements of AI workloads must be carefully considered to ensure fast processing and real-time inference.
- **Reliability:** The reliability of the networking and connectivity solutions must be carefully considered to ensure continuous operation and minimize downtime.
- **Scalability:** The scalability of the networking and connectivity solutions must be carefully considered to ensure they can meet the growing demands of AI workloads.

Networking and connectivity are critical components of AI-ready infrastructure, enabling fast and efficient data transfer between nodes and to/from storage. By understanding the networking and connectivity considerations for AI workloads, IT leaders can build an infrastructure that meets the unique demands of AI applications. In the next section, we'll explore cloud vs. on-premise infrastructure for AI.

CHAPTER 2: THE BUILDING BLOCKS OF AI-READY INFRASTRUCTURE

Cloud vs. On-Premise Infrastructure for AI: Making the Right Choice

The choice between cloud and on-premise infrastructure for AI workloads is a critical decision that depends on several factors, including cost, security, scalability, and control. In this section, we'll explore the considerations for choosing between cloud and on-premise infrastructure for AI.

Cloud Infrastructure for AI

Cloud infrastructure offers several benefits for AI workloads, including:

- **Scalability:** Cloud infrastructure can scale up or down as needed, providing the flexibility to handle changing AI workload demands.
- **Cost Savings:** Cloud infrastructure can reduce capital expenditures and operational expenses, providing a cost-effective solution for AI workloads.
- **Accessibility:** Cloud infrastructure provides global accessibility, enabling teams to collaborate and access AI resources from anywhere.
- **Managed Services:** Cloud providers offer managed services, including AI-specific services, that can simplify the deployment and management of AI workloads.

On-Premise Infrastructure for AI

On-premise infrastructure offers several benefits for AI workloads, including:

- **Control:** On-premise infrastructure provides complete control over the infrastructure, enabling customization and optimization for specific AI workloads.
- **Security:** On-premise infrastructure can enhance security for sensitive AI datasets and models.
- **Compliance:** On-premise infrastructure can ensure compliance with regulations and standards that require data to be stored on-premise.
- **Latency:** On-premise infrastructure can reduce latency for AI workloads that require real-time processing.

Hybrid Infrastructure for AI

Hybrid infrastructure, which combines cloud and on-premise infrastructure, offers several benefits for AI workloads, including:

- **Flexibility:** Hybrid infrastructure provides the flexibility to use cloud infrastructure for certain AI workloads and on-premise infrastructure for others.
- **Scalability:** Hybrid infrastructure can scale up or down as needed, providing the flexibility to handle changing AI workload demands.
- **Cost Savings:** Hybrid infrastructure can reduce capital expendi-

tures and operational expenses, providing a cost-effective solution for AI workloads.
- **Security:** Hybrid infrastructure can enhance security for sensitive AI datasets and models.

Key Considerations for Choosing Between Cloud and On-Premise Infrastructure

When choosing between cloud and on-premise infrastructure for AI workloads, several key considerations must be taken into account:

- **Cost:** The cost of cloud and on-premise infrastructure must be carefully considered, including capital expenditures, operational expenses, and total cost of ownership.
- **Security:** The security requirements of AI workloads must be carefully considered, including data encryption, access controls, and compliance with regulations.
- **Scalability:** The scalability requirements of AI workloads must be carefully considered, including the ability to scale up or down as needed.
- **Control:** The level of control required over the infrastructure must be carefully considered, including customization and optimization for specific AI workloads.
- **Latency:** The latency requirements of AI workloads must be carefully considered, including the need for real-time processing.

The choice between cloud and on-premise infrastructure for AI workloads depends on several factors, including cost, security, scalability, and control. By understanding the benefits and considerations of each option, IT leaders can make informed decisions about the best infrastructure for their AI workloads. In the next chapter, we'll explore transforming IT operations with AI.

Summary and Key Points

In this chapter, we've explored the building blocks of AI-ready infrastructure, including hardware considerations, software-defined infrastructure, data storage and management, networking and connectivity, and cloud vs. on-premise infrastructure for AI. These components are critical to supporting the unique demands of AI workloads.

Summary

The building blocks of AI-ready infrastructure include:

1. **Hardware Considerations:** GPUs, specialized processors, and high-performance computing are necessary for handling the computational demands of AI workloads.
2. **Software-Defined Infrastructure:** SDI enables the automation, orchestration, and management of AI workloads, simplifying infrastructure management and improving resource utilization.
3. **Data Storage and Management:** AI workloads require scalable, high-performance storage solutions that handle diverse data formats and structures.

4. **Networking and Connectivity:** High-bandwidth, low-latency connections are necessary for fast data transfer and processing.
5. **Cloud vs. On-Premise Infrastructure:** The choice between cloud and on-premise infrastructure depends on cost, security, scalability, and control considerations.

Key Points

1. AI workloads require specialized hardware, including GPUs and specialized processors.

2. Software-defined infrastructure simplifies infrastructure management and improves resource utilization.

3. Data storage and management solutions must be scalable, high-performance, and able to handle diverse data formats and structures.

4. Networking and connectivity solutions must provide high-bandwidth, low-latency connections.

5. The choice between cloud and on-premise infrastructure depends on cost, security, scalability, and control considerations.

In the next chapter, we'll explore transforming IT operations with AI, including predictive monitoring, automation, and security. This will provide a detailed understanding of how AI can be leveraged to improve IT operations and drive business success.

II

Part 2: Transforming IT Operations

Chapter 3: From Reactive to Predictive: AI-Powered IT Operations

The Limitations of Traditional IT Operations Management

Traditional IT operations management (ITOM) practices are often reactive, focusing on resolving issues after they occur. This approach can lead to significant downtime, reduced productivity, and increased costs. In this section, we'll explore the limitations of traditional ITOM and how AI can transform IT operations.

Reactive vs. Proactive IT Operations

Traditional ITOM is often reactive, meaning that IT teams respond to issues after they occur. This reactive approach can lead to:

- **Downtime:** Reactive ITOM can result in extended downtime, impacting business operations and revenue.
- **Reduced Productivity:** Reactive ITOM can divert IT resources from

strategic activities, reducing productivity and innovation.
- **Increased Costs:** Reactive ITOM can lead to increased costs due to the need for manual intervention, overtime, and potential hardware or software replacements.

Limitations of Traditional ITOM Tools

Traditional ITOM tools, such as:

- **Monitoring Tools:** Monitoring tools provide real-time visibility into system performance but cannot often predict issues or automate resolution.
- **Ticketing Systems:** Ticketing systems manage incident resolution but can be slow and inefficient, leading to prolonged resolution times.
- **CMDBs:** Configuration Management Databases (CMDBs) track IT assets but often lack real-time data and automated workflows.

The Need for Predictive IT Operations

Predictive IT operations, enabled by AI, can transform ITOM by:

- **Predicting Issues:** AI-powered predictive analytics can identify potential issues before they occur, enabling proactive resolution.
- **Automating Resolution:** AI-powered automation can resolve

issues quickly and efficiently, reducing downtime and improving productivity.
- **Improving Efficiency:** AI-powered ITOM can optimize resource allocation, reducing costs and improving efficiency.

Key Challenges in Adopting Predictive IT Operations

Several challenges must be addressed when adopting predictive IT operations, including:

- **Data Quality:** AI models require high-quality data to make accurate predictions.
- **Integration:** Integrating AI-powered tools with existing ITOM systems can be complex.
- **Skills Gap:** IT teams may require new skills to leverage AI-powered ITOM tools effectively.

Traditional ITOM practices are often reactive, leading to downtime, reduced productivity, and increased costs. AI-powered predictive IT operations can transform ITOM by predicting issues, automating resolution, and improving efficiency. However, adopting predictive IT operations requires addressing challenges such as data quality, integration, and the skills gap. In the next section, we'll explore the role of AIOps in predictive IT operations.

Introducing AIOps: Using AI for Proactive Monitoring, Anomaly Detection, and Automated Remediation

AIOps (Artificial Intelligence for IT Operations) is a set of tools and techniques that leverage AI and machine learning to transform IT operations. In this section, we'll explore the role of AIOps in predictive IT operations, including proactive monitoring, anomaly detection, and automated remediation.

What is AIOps?

AIOps is the application of AI and machine learning to IT operations data to enable proactive monitoring, anomaly detection, and automated remediation. AIOps platforms use data from various sources, including:

- **Monitoring Tools:** Real-time monitoring data from tools like Nagios, Prometheus, and New Relic.
- **Log Data:** Log data from applications, servers, and networks.
- **CMDBs:** Configuration Management Databases (CMDBs) that track IT assets and their relationships.

Proactive Monitoring with AIOps

AIOps platforms use machine learning algorithms to analyze data from various sources, enabling proactive monitoring by:

- **Identifying Patterns:** Identifying patterns in data that may indicate potential issues.
- **Predicting Outages:** Predicting outages based on historical data and real-time monitoring.
- **Detecting Anomalies:** Detecting anomalies in system behavior that may indicate potential issues.

Anomaly Detection with AIOps

AIOps platforms use advanced analytics and machine learning to detect anomalies in system behavior, including:

- **Statistical Analysis:** Statistical analysis of data to identify outliers and anomalies.
- **Machine Learning Models:** Machine learning models that learn normal system behavior and detect deviations.
- **Real-Time Analysis:** Real-time analysis of data to detect anomalies as they occur.

Automated Remediation with AIOps

AIOps platforms can automate remediation by:

- **Automated Workflows:** Automating workflows to resolve issues quickly and efficiently.
- **Self-Healing Systems:** Enabling self-healing systems that can automatically recover from failures.
- **Root Cause Analysis:** Performing root cause analysis to identify and address the underlying causes of issues.

Benefits of AIOps

The benefits of AIOps include:

- **Improved Uptime:** Improved uptime and reduced downtime through proactive monitoring and automated remediation.
- **Increased Efficiency:** Increased efficiency through automation and reduced manual intervention.
- **Enhanced Customer Experience:** Enhanced customer experience through faster issue resolution and improved system reliability.

Key Considerations for Implementing AIOps

Several key considerations must be taken into account when implementing AIOps, including:

- **Data Quality:** Ensuring high-quality data to enable accurate predictions and detections.
- **Integration:** Integrating AIOps platforms with existing ITOM systems and tools.
- **Change Management:** Managing change and ensuring IT teams are prepared to work with AIOps platforms.

AIOps is a critical component of predictive IT operations, enabling proactive monitoring, anomaly detection, and automated remediation. By leveraging AIOps, IT leaders can transform their operations, improving uptime, efficiency, and customer experience. In the next section, we'll explore case studies of successful AIOps implementations.

Case Studies of Successful AIOps Implementations

In this section, we'll explore case studies of successful AIOps implementations, highlighting the benefits and challenges of adopting AIOps in real-world scenarios.

Case Study 1: Predictive Maintenance in Manufacturing

A leading manufacturing company implemented an AIOps platform to predict equipment failures and reduce downtime. The platform used machine learning algorithms to analyze sensor data from equipment, predicting failures with 95% accuracy. This enabled the company to reduce downtime by 80% and save $1 million in maintenance costs annually.

Case Study 2: Automated Incident Resolution in Financial Services

A global financial services company implemented an AIOps platform to automate incident resolution. The platform used natural language processing (NLP) to analyze incident tickets and automatically resolve 70% of incidents without human intervention. This reduced the mean time to resolve (MTTR) by 75% and saved $2 million in operational costs annually.

Case Study 3: Anomaly Detection in E-commerce

An e-commerce company implemented an AIOps platform to detect anomalies in website traffic and prevent outages. The platform used machine learning algorithms to analyze traffic patterns, detecting anomalies in real-time and enabling proactive resolution. This reduced website downtime by 90% and increased revenue by 5%.

Case Study 4: AI-Driven IT Service Management in Healthcare

A healthcare organization implemented an AIOps platform to automate IT service management. The platform used AI-powered chatbots to resolve 80% of user requests without human intervention, reducing the mean time to resolve (MTTR) by 85% and improving user satisfaction by 90%.

Key Takeaways from the Case Studies

- **Predictive Maintenance:** AIOps can predict equipment failures, reducing downtime and maintenance costs.
- **Automated Incident Resolution:** AIOps can automate incident resolution, reducing MTTR and operational costs.
- **Anomaly Detection:** AIOps can detect real-time anomalies, enabling proactive resolution and reducing downtime.
- **AI-Driven IT Service Management:** AIOps can automate IT service management, improving user satisfaction and reducing MTTR.

Lessons Learned from the Case Studies

- **Data Quality:** High-quality data is critical for accurate predictions and detections.
- **Integration:** Integration with existing ITOM systems and tools is essential for successful AIOps implementation.
- **Change Management:** Managing change and ensuring IT teams are prepared to work with AIOps platforms is critical for success.
- **Continuous Improvement:** Monitoring and improving AIOps platforms is necessary to ensure ongoing benefits.

These case studies demonstrate the benefits of AIOps in real-world scenarios, including predictive maintenance, automated incident resolution, anomaly detection, and AI-driven IT service management. By understanding the key takeaways and lessons learned from these case studies, IT leaders can successfully implement AIOps in their organizations. In the next section, we'll explore automating IT infrastructure management with AI.

Summary and Key Points

In this chapter, we've explored the transformation of IT operations from reactive to predictive using AI-powered IT operations. We've discussed the limitations of traditional IT operations management, introduced AIOps, and examined case studies of successful AIOps implementations.

Summary

The chapter has covered:

1. **The Limitations of Traditional IT Operations Management:** The reactive nature of traditional ITOM leads to downtime, reduced productivity, and increased costs.
2. **Introducing AIOps:** Using AI and machine learning to transform IT operations, enabling proactive monitoring, anomaly detection, and automated remediation.
3. **Case Studies of Successful AIOps Implementations:** Real-world examples of AIOps in predictive maintenance, automated incident resolution, anomaly detection, and AI-driven IT service management.

CHAPTER 3: FROM REACTIVE TO PREDICTIVE: AI-POWERED IT...

Key Points

1. Traditional ITOM is reactive, leading to downtime and reduced productivity.

2. AIOps enable proactive monitoring, anomaly detection, and automated remediation.

3. AIOps can predict equipment failures, automate incident resolution, detect anomalies, and drive AI-powered IT service management.

4. Successful AIOps implementation requires high-quality data, integration with existing systems, change management, and continuous improvement.

In the next chapter, we'll explore automating IT infrastructure management with AI, including resource allocation, capacity planning, and incident response. This will provide a detailed understanding of how AI can be leveraged to improve IT infrastructure management and drive business success.

Chapter 4: Automating IT Infrastructure Management with AI

Automating Resource Allocation and Scaling Based on Real-Time Demand

Automating resource allocation and scaling is a critical aspect of AI-driven IT infrastructure management. In this section, we'll explore how AI can automate resource allocation and scaling based on real-time demand, ensuring that IT infrastructure is always optimized for performance and efficiency.

The Need for Real-Time Resource Allocation

Traditional resource allocation methods are often static and inflexible, leading to underutilization or overutilization. Real-time resource allocation, enabled by AI, can:

- **Optimize Resource Utilization:** Ensure that resources are utilized efficiently, reducing waste and improving performance.

- **Improve Scalability:** Scale resources up or down in real-time to meet changing demand, ensuring that IT infrastructure can handle sudden spikes or drops in usage.
- **Enhance Agility:** Enable IT teams to respond quickly to changing business needs, improving agility and competitiveness.

AI-Driven Resource Allocation

AI-driven resource allocation uses machine learning algorithms to analyze real-time data and make decisions about resource allocation. This includes:

- **Predictive Analytics:** Analyzing historical data and real-time metrics to predict future demand and allocate resources accordingly.
- **Real-Time Monitoring:** Continuously monitoring system performance and adjusting resource allocation in real-time to ensure optimal performance.
- **Automated Scaling:** Automatically scaling resources up or down based on real-time demand, ensuring that IT infrastructure is always optimized for performance and efficiency.

Key Technologies for AI-Driven Resource Allocation

Several key technologies are critical for AI-driven resource allocation, including:

- **Cloud Computing:** Cloud computing provides the scalability and flexibility necessary for real-time resource allocation.
- **Containerization:** Containerization technologies like Docker and Kubernetes enable the efficient allocation and scaling of resources.
- **Serverless Computing:** Serverless computing models like AWS Lambda and Azure Functions enable the automated scaling of resources based on real-time demand.

Benefits of AI-Driven Resource Allocation

The benefits of AI-driven resource allocation include:

- **Improved Efficiency:** Resources are utilized more efficiently, reducing waste and improving performance.
- **Enhanced Scalability:** Resources can be scaled up or down in real-time to meet changing demand, ensuring that IT infrastructure can handle sudden spikes or drops in usage.
- **Increased Agility:** IT teams can respond quickly to changing business needs, improving agility and competitiveness.

Challenges and Considerations

Several challenges and considerations must be addressed when implementing AI-driven resource allocation, including:

- **Data Quality:** High-quality data is critical for accurate predictions and decisions.
- **Integration:** Integration with existing IT systems and tools is essential for successful implementation.
- **Security:** Ensuring the security and integrity of AI-driven resource allocation systems is critical.

AI-driven resource allocation is a critical component of automating IT infrastructure management. By leveraging AI and machine learning, IT leaders can ensure that resources are allocated and scaled in real time, optimizing performance, efficiency, and agility. In the next section, we'll explore AI-powered capacity planning and optimization.

AI-Powered Capacity Planning and Optimization

AI-powered capacity planning and optimization are critical components of automating IT infrastructure management. In this section, we'll explore how AI can optimize capacity planning, ensuring that IT infrastructure is always optimized for performance and efficiency.

The Need for AI-Powered Capacity Planning

Traditional capacity planning methods are often manual and reactive, leading to underutilization or overutilization of resources. AI-powered capacity planning can:

- **Predict Capacity Requirements:** Analyze historical data and real-time metrics to predict future capacity requirements.
- **Optimize Resource Allocation:** Optimize resource allocation based on predicted capacity requirements, ensuring that resources are utilized efficiently.
- **Automate Capacity Planning:** Automate the capacity planning process, reducing the need for manual intervention and improving accuracy.

AI-Driven Capacity Planning

AI-driven capacity planning uses machine learning algorithms to analyze data and predict future capacity requirements. This includes:

- **Predictive Analytics:** Analyzing historical data and real-time metrics to predict future capacity requirements.
- **Real-Time Monitoring:** Continuously monitoring system performance and adjusting capacity planning accordingly.
- **Automated Capacity Planning:** Automatically generating capacity plans based on predicted requirements, ensuring that resources are allocated efficiently.

Key Technologies for AI-Driven Capacity Planning

Several key technologies are critical for AI-driven capacity planning, including:

- **Machine Learning:** Machine learning algorithms analyze data and predict future capacity requirements.
- **Cloud Computing:** Cloud computing provides the scalability and flexibility necessary for AI-driven capacity planning.
- **Data Analytics:** Data analytics platforms are used to analyze large datasets and generate insights for capacity planning.

Benefits of AI-Driven Capacity Planning

The benefits of AI-driven capacity planning include:

- **Improved Efficiency:** Resources are utilized more efficiently, reducing waste and improving performance.
- **Enhanced Scalability:** Resources can be scaled up or down in real-time to meet changing demand, ensuring that IT infrastructure can handle sudden spikes or drops in usage.
- **Increased Agility:** IT teams can respond quickly to changing business needs, improving agility and competitiveness.

Challenges and Considerations

Several challenges and considerations must be addressed when implementing AI-driven capacity planning, including:

- **Data Quality:** High-quality data is critical for accurate predictions and decisions.
- **Integration:** Integration with existing IT systems and tools is essential for successful implementation.
- **Security:** Ensuring the security and integrity of AI-driven capacity planning systems is critical.

AI-powered capacity planning and optimization are critical components of automating IT infrastructure management. By leveraging AI and machine learning, IT leaders can ensure that capacity planning is optimized, resources are utilized efficiently, and IT infrastructure is always optimized for performance and efficiency. In the next section, we'll explore intelligent ticketing and automated incident response.

Intelligent Ticketing and Automated Incident Response

Intelligent ticketing and automated incident response are critical components of automating IT infrastructure management. In this section, we'll explore how AI can be used to optimize ticketing and incident response, ensuring that issues are resolved quickly and efficiently.

The Need for Intelligent Ticketing

Traditional ticketing systems are often manual and reactive, leading to delays and inefficiencies in incident resolution. Intelligent ticketing, enabled by AI, can:

- **Automate Ticket Classification:** Automatically classify tickets based on their content, ensuring they are routed to the correct teams and resolved efficiently.
- **Predict Ticket Priority:** Predict the priority of tickets based on their content and historical data, ensuring that critical issues are addressed first.
- **Automate Ticket Routing:** Automatically route tickets to the correct teams and individuals, reducing the need for manual intervention and improving response times.

AI-Driven Ticketing

AI-driven ticketing uses machine learning algorithms to analyze ticket data and decide ticket classification, priority, and routing. This includes:

- **Natural Language Processing (NLP):** Analyzing ticket content using NLP to classify and prioritize tickets automatically.
- **Machine Learning Models:** Using machine learning models to predict ticket priority and routing based on historical data and real-time metrics.

- **Automated Workflows:** Automate workflows to ensure tickets are routed and resolved efficiently.

Automated Incident Response

Automated incident response, enabled by AI, can:

- **Automate Incident Detection:** Automatically detect incidents using real-time monitoring data, identifying issues quickly.
- **Automate Incident Resolution:** Automatically resolve incidents using pre-defined workflows and automation scripts, reducing the need for manual intervention.
- **Automate Incident Reporting:** Automatically generate incident reports, providing insights and recommendations for improvement.

Key Technologies for Intelligent Ticketing and Automated Incident Response

Several key technologies are critical for intelligent ticketing and automated incident response, including:

- **AI-Driven Chatbots:** AI-driven chatbots can automate ticket classification, routing, and resolution, improving user experience and reducing the need for manual intervention.
- **IT Service Management (ITSM) Tools:** ITSM tools like ServiceNow

and BMC Helix ITSM provide the foundation for intelligent ticketing and automated incident response.
- **Automation Platforms:** Automation platforms like Ansible and Puppet enable the automation of incident response workflows.

Benefits of Intelligent Ticketing and Automated Incident Response

The benefits of intelligent ticketing and automated incident response include:

- **Improved Efficiency:** Issues are resolved more quickly and efficiently, reducing downtime and improving user satisfaction.
- **Enhanced Productivity:** IT teams can focus on higher-value tasks, improving productivity and reducing the need for manual intervention.
- **Increased Agility:** Organizations can respond more quickly to changing business needs, improving agility and competitiveness.

Challenges and Considerations

Several challenges and considerations must be addressed when implementing intelligent ticketing and automated incident response, including:

- **Data Quality:** High-quality data is critical for accurate predictions and decisions.
- **Integration:** Integration with existing IT systems and tools is essential for successful implementation.
- **Change Management:** Managing change and ensuring that IT teams are prepared to work with AI-driven ticketing and incident response systems is critical.

Intelligent ticketing and automated incident response are critical components of automating IT infrastructure management. By leveraging AI and machine learning, IT leaders can resolve issues quickly and efficiently, improving user satisfaction, productivity, and agility. In the next section, we'll explore the role of AI in IT service management.

The Role of AI in IT Service Management (ITSM)

AI is transforming IT service management (ITSM) by automating and optimizing various processes, including incident management, problem management, and change management. In this section, we'll explore the role of AI in ITSM, including its applications, benefits, and challenges.

Applications of AI in ITSM

AI is being applied in various areas of ITSM, including:

- **Incident Management:** AI-powered incident management involves the automated detection, classification, and resolution of incidents, reducing the mean time to resolve (MTTR) and improving incident resolution rates.
- **Problem Management:** AI-powered problem management involves the automated identification of root causes, prediction of potential problems, and recommendation of solutions, reducing the mean time to detect (MTTD) and improving problem resolution rates.
- **Change Management:** AI-powered change management involves the automated assessment of change risks, prediction of change outcomes, and recommendation of change strategies, reducing the risk of change failures and improving change success rates.

Benefits of AI in ITSM

The benefits of AI in ITSM include:

- **Improved Efficiency:** AI automates routine tasks, allowing IT staff to focus on higher-value activities, improving efficiency and reducing costs.
- **Enhanced Accuracy:** AI reduces the likelihood of human error, improving the accuracy of incident, problem, and change management processes.
- **Increased Agility:** AI enables faster incident resolution, problem identification, and change implementation, improving agility and responsiveness to business needs.
- **Better Decision-Making:** AI provides insights and recommenda-

tions based on data analysis, enabling better decision-making in ITSM.

Challenges of AI in ITSM

Several challenges must be addressed when implementing AI in ITSM, including:

- **Data Quality:** AI requires high-quality data to make accurate predictions and decisions.
- **Integration:** AI must be integrated with existing ITSM tools and processes, which can be complex and time-consuming.
- **Change Management:** Implementing AI in ITSM requires significant changes to processes and workflows, which can be challenging for IT teams.
- **Skills Gap:** IT teams may require new skills to leverage AI in ITSM effectively.

Key Technologies for AI in ITSM

Several key technologies are critical for AI in ITSM, including:

- **Machine Learning:** Machine learning algorithms are used to analyze data and make predictions in ITSM.
- **Natural Language Processing (NLP):** NLP analyzes incident de-

scriptions, problem statements, and change requests, enabling automated classification and routing.
- **Automation Platforms:** Automation platforms like Ansible and Puppet automate ITSM processes, such as incident resolution and change implementation.

AI transforms ITSM by automating and optimizing various processes, improving efficiency, accuracy, agility, and decision-making. However, implementing AI in ITSM requires careful consideration of data quality, integration, change management, and skills gap challenges. By understanding the role of AI in ITSM, IT leaders can leverage AI to improve IT service delivery and drive business success. In the next chapter, we'll explore securing the AI-powered enterprise.

Summary and Key Points

In this chapter, we've explored the automation of IT infrastructure management with AI, including automating resource allocation and scaling, AI-powered capacity planning and optimization, intelligent ticketing and automated incident response, and the role of AI in IT service management.

Summary

The chapter has covered:

1. **Automating Resource Allocation and Scaling:** AI-driven resource allocation and scaling based on real-time demand, ensuring that resources are utilized efficiently and IT infrastructure is always optimized for performance and efficiency.
2. **AI-Powered Capacity Planning and Optimization:** AI-driven capacity planning and optimization, predicting capacity requirements and optimizing resource allocation, ensuring that resources are utilized efficiently and IT infrastructure is always optimized for performance and efficiency.
3. **Intelligent Ticketing and Automated Incident Response:** AI-driven ticketing and incident response, automating ticket classification, routing, and resolution, and improving incident resolution rates and user satisfaction.
4. **The Role of AI in IT Service Management:** The role of AI in ITSM, including its applications, benefits, and challenges, and how AI is transforming incident management, problem management, and change management.

Key Points

1. AI can automate resource allocation and scaling, improving efficiency and scalability.

2. AI-powered capacity planning and optimization can predict capacity requirements and optimize resource allocation.

3. Intelligent ticketing and automated incident response can improve incident resolution rates and user satisfaction.

CHAPTER 4: AUTOMATING IT INFRASTRUCTURE MANAGEMENT WITH AI

4. AI is transforming ITSM, improving efficiency, accuracy, agility, and decision-making.

In the next chapter, we'll explore securing the AI-powered enterprise, including unique security challenges posed by AI systems, protecting AI models from attacks, securing data pipelines for AI training and inference, and AI-driven threat intelligence and security monitoring. This will provide a detailed understanding of how to secure AI systems and data, ensuring the integrity and confidentiality of AI applications.

Chapter 5: Securing the AI-Powered Enterprise

Unique Security Challenges Posed by AI Systems

AI systems introduce new security challenges that must be addressed to ensure the integrity and confidentiality of AI applications. In this section, we'll explore the unique security challenges AI systems pose, including data poisoning, model inversion, and adversarial attacks.

Data Poisoning

Data poisoning involves manipulating the training data to compromise the integrity of AI models. This can be done by:

- **Inserting Malicious Data:** Inserting malicious data into the training dataset to influence the model's behavior.
- **Modifying Data:** Modifying existing data to alter the model's performance or accuracy.

Model Inversion

Model inversion involves using an AI model to infer sensitive information about the training data. This can be done by:

- **Reconstructing Training Data:** Reconstructing the training data from the model's parameters.
- **Inferring Sensitive Information:** Inferring sensitive information about the training data, such as personal identifiable information (PII).

Adversarial Attacks

Adversarial attacks involve manipulating the input data to cause the AI model to misbehave or make incorrect predictions. This can be done by:

- **Adding Noise:** Adding noise to the input data causes the model to misclassify or mispredict.
- **Generating Adversarial Examples:** Generating adversarial examples designed to cause the model to fail.

Other Security Challenges

Other security challenges posed by AI systems include:

- **Model Stealing:** Stealing AI models or intellectual property.
- **Data Exfiltration:** Exfiltrating sensitive data used to train AI models.
- **Model Tampering:** Tampering with AI models to alter their behavior or performance.

Key Considerations for Securing AI Systems

Several key considerations must be taken into account when securing AI systems, including:

- **Data Quality:** Ensuring the quality and integrity of the training data.
- **Model Validation:** Validating AI models to ensure they are accurate and reliable.
- **Access Control:** Implementing access controls to prevent unauthorized access to AI models and data.
- **Encryption:** Encrypting data and models to prevent unauthorized access or use.

AI systems introduce new security challenges that must be addressed to ensure the integrity and confidentiality of AI applications. By understanding these challenges and considering key considerations,

IT leaders can ensure the security of AI systems and protect against data poisoning, model inversion, adversarial attacks, and other security threats. In the next section, we'll explore protecting AI models from attacks.

Protecting AI Models from Attacks

Protecting AI models from attacks is critical to ensuring the integrity and confidentiality of AI applications. In this section, we'll explore the methods for protecting AI models from data poisoning and adversarial examples.

Data Poisoning Protection

Data poisoning involves manipulating the training data to compromise the integrity of AI models. To protect against data poisoning, several methods can be employed:

- **Data Validation:** Validating the training data to ensure accuracy and reliability.
- **Data Cleansing:** Cleansing the training data to remove any malicious or erroneous data.
- **Data Encryption:** Encrypting the training data to prevent unauthorized access or modification.
- **Anomaly Detection:** Implementing anomaly detection techniques to identify and remove anomalous data points.

Adversarial Examples Protection

Adversarial examples involve manipulating the input data to cause the AI model to misbehave or make incorrect predictions. To protect against adversarial examples, several methods can be employed:

- **Adversarial Training:** Training AI models on adversarial examples to improve their robustness.
- **Input Preprocessing:** Preprocessing the input data to detect and remove adversarial examples.
- **Model Ensembling:** Using model ensembling techniques to improve the robustness of AI models against adversarial examples.
- **Defensive Distillation:** Using defensive distillation techniques to improve the robustness of AI models against adversarial examples.

Other Protection Methods

Other methods for protecting AI models from attacks include:

- **Model Pruning:** Pruning AI models to reduce their complexity and improve their robustness.
- **Regularization Techniques:** Using regularization techniques to improve the robustness of AI models.
- **Differential Privacy:** Implementing differential privacy techniques to protect the privacy of the training data.
- **Explainability Techniques:** Using explainability techniques to understand how AI models make predictions and identify potential

vulnerabilities.

Key Considerations for Protecting AI Models

Several key considerations must be taken into account when protecting AI models from attacks, including:

- **Model Complexity:** The complexity of the AI model can impact its robustness against attacks.
- **Data Quality:** The quality of the training data can impact the robustness of the AI model.
- **Model Interpretability:** The interpretability of the AI model can impact its robustness against attacks.
- **Continuous Monitoring:** Continuously monitoring AI models for signs of attack or compromise.

Protecting AI models from data poisoning and adversarial examples is critical to ensuring the integrity and confidentiality of AI applications. By employing various protection methods and considering key factors, IT leaders can ensure the security and reliability of AI models. In the next section, we'll explore securing data pipelines for AI training and inference.

Securing Data Pipelines for AI Training and Inference

Securing data pipelines for AI training and inference is critical to ensuring the integrity and confidentiality of AI applications. In this section, we'll explore the methods for securing data pipelines, including data encryption, access control, and data masking.

Data Encryption

Data encryption is a critical component of securing data pipelines. This involves:

- **In-Transit Encryption:** Encrypting data in transit between systems and applications.
- **At-Rest Encryption:** Encrypting data at rest in storage systems.
- **Homomorphic Encryption:** Encrypting data in a way that allows computations to be performed on the encrypted data.

Access Control

Access control is essential for securing data pipelines. This involves:

- **Role-Based Access Control (RBAC):** Implementing RBAC to ensure that only authorized personnel have access to sensitive data.
- **Attribute-Based Access Control (ABAC):** Implementing ABAC to

ensure that access is granted based on user attributes and data attributes.
- **Multi-Factor Authentication (MFA):** Implementing MFA ensures that only authorized personnel can access sensitive data.

Data Masking

Data masking involves obscuring sensitive data to prevent unauthorized access. This includes:

- **Data Anonymization:** Anonymizing data to remove identifiable information.
- **Data Pseudonymization:** Pseudonymizing data to replace identifiable information with artificial identifiers.
- **Data Encryption:** Encrypting data to prevent unauthorized access.

Data Loss Prevention (DLP)

DLP involves monitoring and controlling data in motion, in use, and at rest to prevent unauthorized data exfiltration. This includes:

- **Network DLP:** Monitoring network traffic to detect and prevent unauthorized data exfiltration.
- **Endpoint DLP:** Monitoring endpoint devices to detect and prevent unauthorized data exfiltration.

- **Storage DLP:** Monitoring storage systems to detect and prevent unauthorized data exfiltration.

Key Considerations for Securing Data Pipelines

Several key considerations must be taken into account when securing data pipelines, including:

- **Data Classification:** Classifying data based on its sensitivity and confidentiality requirements.
- **Data Flow Mapping:** Mapping data flows to identify potential vulnerabilities and security risks.
- **Compliance Regulations:** Ensuring compliance with relevant regulations, such as GDPR and HIPAA.
- **Continuous Monitoring:** Continuously monitoring data pipelines for signs of attack or compromise.

Securing data pipelines for AI training and inference is critical to ensuring the integrity and confidentiality of AI applications. By employing data encryption, access control, data masking, and DLP and considering key factors, IT leaders can ensure the security and reliability of AI data pipelines. In the next section, we'll explore AI-driven threat intelligence and security monitoring.

CHAPTER 5: SECURING THE AI-POWERED ENTERPRISE

AI-Driven Threat Intelligence and Security Monitoring

AI-driven threat intelligence and security monitoring are critical to securing the AI-powered enterprise. In this section, we'll explore how AI can enhance threat intelligence and security monitoring, including anomaly detection, threat prediction, and incident response.

Anomaly Detection

AI-powered anomaly detection involves using machine learning algorithms to identify unusual patterns in system behavior that may indicate a security threat. This includes:

- **Real-Time Monitoring:** Continuously monitoring system logs and network traffic in real-time to detect anomalies.
- **Machine Learning Models:** Using machine learning models to analyze data and identify anomalies.
- **Threshold-Based Detection:** Setting thresholds for normal behavior and detecting anomalies that exceed these thresholds.

Threat Prediction

AI-powered threat prediction uses machine learning algorithms to predict potential security threats based on historical data and real-time metrics. This includes:

- **Predictive Analytics:** Analyzing historical data and real-time metrics to predict potential security threats.
- **Threat Modeling:** Modeling potential threats to identify vulnerabilities and predict potential attack vectors.
- **Risk Assessment:** Assessing the risk of potential threats to prioritize security efforts.

Incident Response

AI-powered incident response involves using machine learning algorithms to automate and optimize incident response processes. This includes:

- **Automated Incident Detection:** Automatically detecting incidents based on anomaly detection and threat prediction.
- **Automated Incident Response:** Automatically responding to incidents based on pre-defined workflows and playbooks.
- **Incident Analysis:** Analyzing incidents to identify root causes and improve incident response processes.

Key Technologies for AI-Driven Threat Intelligence and Security Monitoring

Several key technologies are critical for AI-driven threat intelligence and security monitoring, including:

- **Machine Learning:** Machine learning algorithms analyze data, identify anomalies, and predict threats.
- **Natural Language Processing (NLP):** NLP is used to analyze threat intelligence feeds and identify potential threats.
- **Cloud-Based Security Information and Event Management (SIEM) Systems:** Cloud-based SIEM systems provide real-time monitoring and analysis of security-related data.

Benefits of AI-Driven Threat Intelligence and Security Monitoring

The benefits of AI-driven threat intelligence and security monitoring include:

- **Improved Detection:** AI-powered anomaly detection and threat prediction improve the detection of security threats.
- **Faster Response:** AI-powered incident response automates and optimizes incident response processes, reducing response times.
- **Enhanced Security:** AI-driven threat intelligence and security monitoring enhance overall security by identifying vulnerabilities and predicting potential threats.

Challenges and Considerations

Several challenges and considerations must be addressed when implementing AI-driven threat intelligence and security monitoring, including:

- **Data Quality:** High-quality data is critical for accurate anomaly detection and threat prediction.
- **Integration:** Integration with security systems and tools is essential for successful implementation.
- **Change Management:** Managing change and ensuring that security teams are prepared to work with AI-driven threat intelligence and security monitoring systems is critical.

AI-driven threat intelligence and security monitoring are critical to securing the AI-powered enterprise. By leveraging AI and machine learning, IT leaders can improve threat detection, response times, and security. In the next section, we'll explore the future of AI in IT operations.

Summary and Key Points

In this chapter, we've explored securing the AI-powered enterprise, including unique security challenges posed by AI systems, protecting AI models from attacks, securing data pipelines for AI training and inference, and AI-driven threat intelligence and security monitoring.

CHAPTER 5: SECURING THE AI-POWERED ENTERPRISE

Summary

The chapter has covered:

1. **Unique Security Challenges:** The unique security challenges AI systems pose include data poisoning, model inversion, and adversarial attacks.
2. **Protecting AI Models:** Protecting AI models from attacks, including data poisoning and adversarial examples.
3. **Securing Data Pipelines:** Securing data pipelines for AI training and inference, including data encryption, access control, and data masking.
4. **AI-Driven Threat Intelligence and Security Monitoring:** AI-driven threat intelligence and security monitoring, including anomaly detection, threat prediction, and incident response.

Key Points

1. AI systems introduce new security challenges that must be addressed.

2. Protecting AI models from attacks is critical to ensuring the integrity and confidentiality of AI applications.

3. Securing data pipelines for AI training and inference is essential to prevent unauthorized access or modification of sensitive data.

4. AI-driven threat intelligence and security monitoring can improve

threat detection, response times, and overall security.

In the next chapter, we'll explore the future of AI in IT operations, including the potential of AI to transform IT operations, the role of AI in digital transformation, and the skills and competencies required for AI-driven IT operations. This will provide a detailed understanding of how AI will continue to shape the future of IT operations.

III

Part 3: Aligning IT with Business Transformation

Chapter 6: Data: The Lifeblood of AI and the Modern Enterprise

The Critical Importance of Data Quality, Governance, and Management for AI

Data is the lifeblood of AI and the modern enterprise, and its quality, governance, and management are critical to the success of AI initiatives. In this section, we'll explore the importance of data quality, governance, and management for AI, including data preparation, data governance, and data management.

Data Preparation for AI

Data preparation is a critical step in the AI lifecycle, involving the collection, cleaning, transformation, and preparation of data for AI model training. This includes:

- **Data Ingestion:** Ingesting data from various sources, including structured and unstructured data.

- **Data Cleaning:** Cleaning data to remove errors, inconsistencies, and missing values.
- **Data Transformation:** Transforming data into formats suitable for AI model training.
- **Data Augmentation:** Augmenting data to increase its size and diversity.

Data Governance for AI

Data governance is essential for ensuring the quality, security, and compliance of data used in AI initiatives. This includes:

- **Data Classification:** Classifying data based on its sensitivity and confidentiality requirements.
- **Data Access Control:** Implementing access controls to ensure that only authorized personnel have access to sensitive data.
- **Data Lineage:** Tracking the origin, movement, and transformation of data to ensure transparency and auditability.
- **Data Quality Metrics:** Establishing data quality metrics to ensure data meets the required standards for AI model training.

Data Management for AI

Data management is critical for ensuring the efficient and effective use of data in AI initiatives. This includes:

- **Data Storage:** Storing data in scalable and secure storage solutions, such as data lakes and data warehouses.
- **Data Retrieval:** Retrieving data efficiently and effectively for AI model training and inference.
- **Data Versioning:** Managing different versions of data to ensure reproducibility and auditability.
- **Data Security:** Ensuring the security and integrity of data throughout its lifecycle.

Key Considerations for Data Quality, Governance, and Management

Several key considerations must be taken into account when ensuring data quality, governance, and management for AI, including:

- **Data Quality:** Ensuring data is accurate, complete, and consistent.
- **Data Governance:** Ensuring data governance policies and procedures are followed.
- **Data Management:** Ensuring data is efficiently and effectively managed throughout its lifecycle.
- **Scalability:** Ensuring data management solutions can scale to meet the growing demands of AI initiatives.

Data quality, governance, and management are critical components of AI success. By ensuring data is of high quality, governed effectively, and managed efficiently, IT leaders can ensure the success of AI initiatives and drive business transformation. In the next section, we'll explore the role of AI in digital transformation.

Building a Data-Centric Infrastructure: Data Lakes, Data Warehouses, and Data Pipelines

Building a data-centric infrastructure is critical to supporting AI initiatives and driving business transformation. In this section, we'll explore the components of a data-centric infrastructure, including data lakes, data warehouses, and data pipelines.

Data Lakes

Data lakes are centralized repositories that store all types of data in their native format, including structured, semi-structured, and unstructured data. Key characteristics of data lakes include:

- **Schema-on-Read:** Data lakes store data in its native format, with schema applied at query time.
- **Scalability:** Data lakes are designed to handle large volumes of data and scale horizontally.
- **Flexibility:** Data lakes support various data formats and can handle real-time data ingestion.

Data Warehouses

Data warehouses are structured repositories that store data in a predefined schema optimized for querying and analysis. Key characteristics of data warehouses include:

- **Schema-on-Write:** Data warehouses store data in a predefined schema, with data transformed and loaded into the warehouse.
- **Optimized for Querying:** Data warehouses are optimized for querying and analysis, with data organized for fast query performance.
- **Structured Data:** Data warehouses typically store structured data, such as relational data.

Data Pipelines

Data pipelines extract, transform, and load data from various sources to a target system, such as a data lake or data warehouse. Key characteristics of data pipelines include:

- **Data Ingestion:** Data pipelines ingest data from various sources, including APIs, files, and databases.
- **Data Transformation:** Data pipelines transform data into a format suitable for analysis or AI model training.
- **Data Loading:** Data pipelines load data into a target system, such as a data lake or data warehouse.

Building a Data-Centric Infrastructure

Building a data-centric infrastructure involves several key steps, including:

- **Data Strategy:** Developing a data strategy that aligns with business objectives.
- **Data Architecture:** Designing a data architecture that includes data lakes, warehouses, and pipelines.
- **Data Governance:** Implementing policies and procedures to ensure data quality and security.
- **Data Management:** Managing data throughout its lifecycle, including data ingestion, transformation, and loading.

Key Technologies for Building a Data-Centric Infrastructure

Several key technologies are critical for building a data-centric infrastructure, including:

- **Hadoop and Spark:** Hadoop and Spark are used to build data lakes and pipelines.
- **Cloud-Based Data Warehouses:** Cloud-based data warehouses, such as Amazon Redshift and Google BigQuery, are used for building scalable and secure data warehouses.
- **Data Integration Tools:** Data integration tools, such as Talend and Informatica, are used for building data pipelines.

Benefits of a Data-Centric Infrastructure

The benefits of a data-centric infrastructure include:

- **Improved Data Management:** A data-centric infrastructure improves data management by providing a single, unified view of data.
- **Enhanced Analytics:** A data-centric infrastructure enhances analytics by providing fast and scalable access to data.
- **AI-Ready Data:** A data-centric infrastructure provides AI-ready data, enabling the development of AI models.

Building a data-centric infrastructure is critical to supporting AI initiatives and driving business transformation. By understanding the components of a data-centric infrastructure, including data lakes, data warehouses, and data pipelines, IT leaders can ensure that their organizations have the data foundation necessary for AI success. In the next section, we'll explore the role of AI in digital transformation.

Ensuring Data Security and Privacy in the Age of AI

Ensuring data security and privacy is critical in the age of AI, as AI models rely on vast amounts of data to learn and make decisions. In this section, we'll explore the importance of data security and privacy in AI, including data encryption, access control, and privacy regulations.

Data Encryption

Data encryption is a critical component of data security, using algorithms to protect data from unauthorized access. This includes:

- **In-Transit Encryption:** Encrypting data in transit between systems and applications.
- **At-Rest Encryption:** Encrypting data at rest in storage systems.
- **Homomorphic Encryption:** Encrypting data in a way that allows computations to be performed on the encrypted data.

Access Control

Access control ensures that only authorized personnel can access sensitive data. This includes:

- **Role-Based Access Control (RBAC):** Implementing RBAC to ensure access is granted based on user roles.
- **Attribute-Based Access Control (ABAC):** Implementing ABAC to ensure that access is granted based on user attributes and data attributes.
- **Multi-Factor Authentication (MFA):** Implementing MFA ensures that only authorized personnel can access sensitive data.

Privacy Regulations

Privacy regulations, such as GDPR and CCPA, are critical for ensuring personal data privacy. This includes:

- **Data Minimization:** Minimizing the collection and storage of personal data.
- **Data Anonymization:** Anonymizing data to remove identifiable information.
- **Data Pseudonymization:** Pseudonymizing data to replace identifiable information with artificial identifiers.

Key Considerations for Data Security and Privacy

Several key considerations must be taken into account when ensuring data security and privacy in AI, including:

- **Data Classification:** Classifying data based on its sensitivity and confidentiality requirements.
- **Data Flow Mapping:** Mapping data flows to identify potential vulnerabilities and security risks.
- **Compliance Regulations:** Ensuring compliance with relevant regulations, such as GDPR and CCPA.
- **Continuous Monitoring:** Continuously monitoring data security and privacy to identify potential risks and vulnerabilities.

AI-Driven Data Security and Privacy

AI can be used to enhance data security and privacy, including:

- **Anomaly Detection:** Using AI-powered anomaly detection to identify potential security threats.
- **Predictive Analytics:** Using predictive analytics to predict potential security risks and vulnerabilities.
- **Automated Incident Response:** Using AI-powered automated incident response to respond to security incidents quickly.

Ensuring data security and privacy is critical in the age of AI, as AI models rely on vast amounts of data to learn and make decisions. By employing data encryption, access control, and privacy regulations and leveraging AI-driven data security and privacy, IT leaders can ensure the security and privacy of data. In the next section, we'll explore the role of AI in digital transformation.

Summary and Key Points

In this chapter, we've explored the critical importance of data quality, governance, and management for AI, including building a data-centric infrastructure and ensuring data security and privacy in the age of AI.

Summary

The chapter has covered:

1. **Data Quality, Governance, and Management:** The critical importance of data quality, governance, and management for AI success.
2. **Building a Data-Centric Infrastructure:** Building a data-centric infrastructure, including data lakes, data warehouses, and data pipelines.
3. **Ensuring Data Security and Privacy:** Ensuring data security and privacy in the age of AI, including data encryption, access control, and privacy regulations.

Key Points

1. Data is the lifeblood of AI and the modern enterprise.

2. Data quality, governance, and management are critical to AI success.

3. A data-centric infrastructure, including data lakes, data warehouses, and data pipelines, is essential for AI.

4. Ensuring data security and privacy is critical in the age of AI, including data encryption, access control, and privacy regulations.

In the next chapter, we'll explore the role of AI in digital transformation, including how AI is transforming business models, the role of AI in customer experience, and the future of work in an AI-driven economy. This will provide a detailed understanding of how AI drives business transformation and the implications for IT leaders.

Chapter 7: AI-as-a-Service: Strategies for Adoption and Integration

Understanding the Different Types of AIaaS Offerings

AI-as-a-Service (AIaaS) is a cloud-based service model that provides AI capabilities on-demand, enabling organizations to leverage AI without the need for significant upfront investments in infrastructure, talent, or technology. In this section, we'll explore the different types of AIaaS offerings, including machine learning, natural language processing, computer vision, and predictive analytics.

Machine Learning as a Service (MLaaS)

MLaaS provides machine learning capabilities on-demand, enabling organizations to build, train, and deploy machine learning models without significant upfront investments. Key features of MLaaS include:

- **Model Training:** Training machine learning models using cloud-based infrastructure and algorithms.

- **Model Deployment:** Deploying trained models into production environments.
- **Model Management:** Managing the lifecycle of machine learning models, including versioning, monitoring, and updating.

Natural Language Processing as a Service (NLPaaS)

NLPaaS provides natural language processing capabilities on-demand, enabling organizations to analyze and understand natural language data. Key features of NLPaaS include:

- **Text Analysis:** Analyzing text data to extract insights and meaning.
- **Sentiment Analysis:** Analyzing text data to determine sentiment and emotion.
- **Language Translation:** Translating text data from one language to another.

Computer Vision as a Service (CVaaS)

CVaaS provides computer vision capabilities on-demand, enabling organizations to analyze and understand visual data. Key features of CVaaS include:

- **Image Recognition:** Recognizing objects, people, and patterns within images.

- **Object Detection:** Detecting objects within images and videos.
- **Image Classification:** Classifying images into predefined categories.

Predictive Analytics as a Service (PAaaS)

PAaaS provides predictive analytics capabilities on-demand, enabling organizations to analyze data and make predictions about future outcomes. Key features of PAaaS include:

- **Data Analysis:** Analyzing large datasets to identify patterns and trends.
- **Model Building:** Building predictive models using machine learning algorithms.
- **Forecasting:** Making predictions about future outcomes based on historical data and trends.

Other AIaaS Offerings

Other AIaaS offerings include:

- **Chatbots as a Service (CaaS):** Providing chatbot capabilities on-demand, enabling organizations to automate customer service and support.
- **Speech Recognition as a Service (SRaaS):** Providing speech recog-

nition capabilities on-demand, enabling organizations to analyze and understand spoken language.
- **Robotics Process Automation as a Service (RPaaS):** Providing robotics process automation capabilities on-demand, enabling organizations to automate repetitive tasks and processes.

Key Considerations for AIaaS Adoption

Several key considerations must be taken into account when adopting AIaaS, including:

- **Security:** Ensuring the security and integrity of data and models in the cloud.
- **Integration:** Integrating AIaaS offerings with existing systems and applications.
- **Scalability:** Ensuring AIaaS offerings can scale to meet changing business needs.
- **Cost:** Understanding the cost implications of AIaaS adoption and ensuring cost-effectiveness.

AIaaS offers a range of benefits, including reduced costs, increased scalability, and improved agility. By understanding the different types of AIaaS offerings and key considerations for adoption, IT leaders can make informed decisions about leveraging AIaaS to drive business transformation. In the next section, we'll explore strategies for adopting and integrating AIaaS into existing IT infrastructure.

Evaluating AIaaS Providers and Solutions

Evaluating AIaaS providers and solutions is a critical step in adopting and integrating AIaaS into existing IT infrastructure. In this section, we'll explore the key factors to consider when evaluating AIaaS providers and solutions, including functionality, scalability, security, and cost.

Functionality

Evaluating the functionality of AIaaS providers and solutions involves assessing their capabilities in areas such as:

- **Machine Learning:** The ability to build, train, and deploy machine learning models.
- **Natural Language Processing:** The ability to analyze and understand natural language data.
- **Computer Vision:** The ability to analyze and understand visual data.
- **Predictive Analytics:** The ability to analyze data and predict future outcomes.

Scalability

Evaluating the scalability of AIaaS providers and solutions involves assessing their ability to:

- **Handle Large Datasets:** Process and analyze large datasets efficiently.
- **Scale with Business Needs:** Scale up or down to meet changing business needs.
- **Support Real-Time Processing:** Support real-time processing and analysis of data.

Security

Evaluating the security of AIaaS providers and solutions involves assessing their:

- **Data Encryption:** Use of encryption to protect data in transit and at rest.
- **Access Control:** Implementation of access controls to ensure only authorized personnel have access to data and models.
- **Compliance:** Compliance with relevant regulations, such as GDPR and CCPA.

Cost

Evaluating the cost of AIaaS providers and solutions involves assessing the following:

- **Subscription Models:** The cost of subscription models, including pay-per-use and flat-fee models.
- **Customization Costs:** The cost of customizing AIaaS solutions to meet specific business needs.
- **Integration Costs:** The cost of integrating AIaaS solutions with existing systems and applications.

Integration

Evaluating the integration capabilities of AIaaS providers and solutions involves assessing their:

- **APIs and SDKs:** The availability and quality of APIs and SDKs for integration with existing systems and applications.
- **Pre-Built Integrations:** The availability of pre-built integrations with popular platforms and tools.
- **Custom Integration:** The ability to customize integrations to meet specific business needs.

Support and Services

Evaluating the support and services offered by AIaaS providers involves assessing the following:

- **Documentation and Training:** The quality and availability of documentation and training resources.
- **Support Channels:** The availability and responsiveness of support channels, including phone, email, and chat.
- **Professional Services:** The availability of professional services, such as consulting and implementation services.

Key Considerations for Evaluating AIaaS Providers

Several key considerations must be taken into account when evaluating AIaaS providers, including:

- **Business Needs:** Aligning AIaaS solutions with specific business needs and objectives.
- **Technical Requirements:** Ensuring AIaaS solutions meet technical requirements, such as scalability and security.
- **Vendor Lock-In:** Avoiding vendor lock-in by ensuring solutions are flexible and adaptable.
- **Future Roadmap:** Evaluating the future roadmap of AIaaS providers and their commitment to innovation and improvement.

Evaluating AIaaS providers and solutions is a critical step in adopting and integrating AIaaS into existing IT infrastructure. By considering functionality, scalability, security, cost, integration, support, and services, IT leaders can decide which AIaaS solutions to adopt and how to integrate them effectively. In the next section, we'll explore strategies for integrating AIaaS into existing IT infrastructure.

Integrating AIaaS into Existing IT Infrastructure and Workflows

Integrating AIaaS into existing IT infrastructure and workflows is critical to ensuring seamless adoption and maximizing the benefits of AIaaS. In this section, we'll explore the strategies for integrating AIaaS, including API integration, data integration, and workflow integration.

API Integration

API integration involves integrating AIaaS solutions with existing systems and applications using APIs. This includes:

- **API Design:** Designing APIs that are secure, scalable, and easy to use.
- **API Documentation:** Providing clear and comprehensive API documentation.
- **API Testing:** Testing APIs to ensure they meet performance and security requirements.

Data Integration

Data integration involves integrating AIaaS solutions with existing data sources and systems. This includes:

- **Data Ingestion:** Ingesting data from various sources into AIaaS solutions.
- **Data Transformation:** Transforming data into formats suitable for AIaaS solutions.
- **Data Quality:** Ensuring data quality and integrity throughout the integration process.

Workflow Integration

Workflow integration involves integrating AIaaS solutions into existing business workflows and processes. This includes:

- **Process Mapping:** Mapping business processes to identify areas where AIaaS can add value.
- **Workflow Automation:** Automating workflows using AIaaS solutions.
- **Change Management:** Managing change and ensuring users are trained and prepared to work with AIaaS solutions.

Key Considerations for Integration

Several key considerations must be taken into account when integrating AIaaS into existing IT infrastructure and workflows, including:

- **Security:** Ensuring the security and integrity of data and models during integration.
- **Scalability:** Ensuring that AIaaS solutions can scale to meet changing business needs.
- **Interoperability:** Ensuring that AIaaS solutions can interoperate with existing systems and applications.
- **Change Management:** Managing change and ensuring users are prepared to work with AIaaS solutions.

Integration Strategies

Several integration strategies can be employed, including:

- **Tight Integration:** Integrating AIaaS solutions tightly with existing systems and applications.
- **Loose Integration:** Integrating AIaaS solutions loosely with existing systems and applications.
- **Hybrid Integration:** Integrating AIaaS solutions using tight and loose integration strategies.

Best Practices for Integration

Several best practices for integrating AIaaS into existing IT infrastructure and workflows include:

- **Start Small:** Starting with small-scale integrations and scaling up.
- **Monitor and Analyze:** Continuously monitoring and analyzing integration performance.
- **Collaborate with Stakeholders:** Collaborating with stakeholders to ensure integration meets business needs.
- **Plan for Change:** Planning for change and ensuring that integration is flexible and adaptable.

Integrating AIaaS into existing IT infrastructure and workflows is critical to ensuring seamless adoption and maximizing the benefits of AIaaS. By employing API integration, data integration, and workflow integration strategies and considering key considerations and best practices, IT leaders can ensure successful integration and drive business transformation. In the next section, we'll explore the future of AIaaS and its implications for IT leaders.

Managing Costs and Ensuring ROI from AIaaS Investments

Managing costs and ensuring a return on investment (ROI) from AIaaS investments is critical to ensuring the financial viability of AI initiatives. In this section, we'll explore the strategies for managing costs and ensuring ROI from AIaaS investments, including cost modeling, ROI analysis, and cost optimization.

Cost Modeling

Cost modeling involves estimating the costs associated with AIaaS investments, including:

- **Subscription Costs:** The cost of subscribing to AIaaS solutions.
- **Customization Costs:** The cost of customizing AIaaS solutions to meet specific business needs.
- **Integration Costs:** The cost of integrating AIaaS solutions with existing systems and applications.
- **Training and Support Costs:** The cost of training and supporting users of AIaaS solutions.

ROI Analysis

ROI analysis involves evaluating the financial benefits of AIaaS investments, including:

- **Revenue Growth:** The potential revenue growth resulting from AIaaS investments.
- **Cost Savings:** The potential cost savings resulting from AIaaS investments.
- **Productivity Gains:** The potential productivity gains resulting from AIaaS investments.
- **Competitive Advantage:** The potential competitive advantage resulting from AIaaS investments.

Cost Optimization

Cost optimization involves minimizing the costs associated with AIaaS investments, including:

- **Right-Sizing:** Ensuring that AIaaS solutions are right-sized for business needs.
- **Scalability:** Ensuring that AIaaS solutions can scale up or down to meet changing business needs.
- **Automation:** Automating processes to reduce manual intervention and costs.
- **Efficiency Gains:** Identifying and implementing efficiency gains to reduce costs.

Key Considerations for Managing Costs and Ensuring ROI

Several key considerations must be taken into account when managing costs and ensuring ROI from AIaaS investments, including:

- **Business Case:** Developing a clear business case for AIaaS investments.
- **Cost Transparency:** Ensuring cost transparency throughout the AIaaS investment lifecycle.
- **ROI Metrics:** Establishing clear ROI metrics to measure the success of AIaaS investments.
- **Continuous Monitoring:** Continuously monitoring costs and ROI to ensure alignment with business objectives.

Best Practices for Managing Costs and Ensuring ROI

Several best practices for managing costs and ensuring ROI from AIaaS investments include:

- **Start Small:** Starting with small-scale AIaaS investments and scaling up.
- **Pilot Projects:** Conducting pilot projects to test AIaaS solutions and measure ROI.
- **Collaborate with Stakeholders:** Collaborate with stakeholders to ensure alignment with business objectives.
- **Regular Review:** Regularly reviewing costs and ROI to ensure alignment with business objectives.

Managing costs and ensuring ROI from AIaaS investments is critical to ensuring the financial viability of AI initiatives. By employing cost modeling, ROI analysis, and cost optimization strategies and considering key considerations and best practices, IT leaders can ensure that AIaaS investments deliver tangible business value. In the next section, we'll explore the future of AIaaS and its implications for IT leaders.

Summary and Key Points

In this chapter, we've explored AI-as-a-Service (AIaaS) strategies for adoption and integration, including understanding the different types of AIaaS offerings, evaluating AIaaS providers and solutions, integrating AIaaS into existing IT infrastructure and workflows, and managing costs and ensuring ROI from AIaaS investments.

Summary

The chapter has covered:

1. **Understanding AIaaS Offerings:** Different AIaaS offerings include machine learning, natural language processing, computer vision, and predictive analytics.
2. **Evaluating AIaaS Providers:** Evaluating AIaaS providers and solutions based on functionality, scalability, security, cost, integration, support, and services.
3. **Integrating AIaaS:** Integrating AIaaS into existing IT infrastruc-

ture and workflows, including API integration, data integration, and workflow integration.
4. **Managing Costs and Ensuring ROI:** Managing costs and ensuring ROI from AIaaS investments, including cost modeling, ROI analysis, and cost optimization.

Key Points

1. AIaaS offers a range of benefits, including reduced costs, increased scalability, and improved agility.

2. Evaluating AIaaS providers and solutions is critical to aligning with business needs.

3. Integrating AIaaS into IT infrastructure and workflows requires careful planning and execution.

4. Managing costs and ensuring ROI from AIaaS investments is critical to ensuring the financial viability of AI initiatives.

In the next chapter, we'll explore the future of AI and its implications for IT leaders, including the potential of AI to transform industries, the role of AI in digital transformation, and the skills and competencies required for AI-driven IT operations. This will provide a detailed understanding of how AI will continue to shape the future of IT operations and the implications for IT leaders.

Chapter 8: The Evolving Role of IT in the AI-Driven Organization

From Cost Center to Strategic Business Enabler

The role of IT is evolving from a cost center to a strategic business enabler in the AI-driven organization. In this section, we'll explore how IT leaders can leverage AI to drive business transformation and become strategic partners to the business.

The Traditional Role of IT

Traditionally, IT has been viewed as a cost center, focused on maintaining and supporting existing systems and infrastructure. This includes:

- **Keeping the Lights On:** Ensuring the continued operation of existing systems and infrastructure.
- **Managing Costs:** Managing the costs associated with IT operations, including hardware, software, and personnel.
- **Providing Support:** Support end-users and ensure that IT services

are available and reliable.

The Evolving Role of IT

The evolving role of IT involves leveraging AI to drive business transformation and become a strategic business enabler. This includes:

- Driving Innovation: Driving innovation through AI and other emerging technologies.
- **Enabling Business Outcomes:** Enabling business outcomes through the strategic use of AI and IT.
- **Partnering with the Business:** Partnering with the business to understand its needs and develop solutions that meet them.

Key Skills and Competencies for IT Leaders

Several key skills and competencies are required for IT leaders to succeed in the AI-driven organization, including:

- **Business Acumen:** Understanding the business and its needs.
- **Technical Expertise:** Having technical expertise in AI and other emerging technologies.
- **Strategic Thinking:** Thinking strategically about how AI can drive business transformation.
- **Communication Skills:** Communicating effectively with the busi-

ness and other stakeholders.

The Future of IT Leadership

The future of IT leadership involves:

- **Leading by Example:** Leading by example and demonstrating the value of AI and other emerging technologies.
- **Developing Talent:** Developing talent and ensuring IT teams have the skills and competencies to succeed in the AI-driven organization.
- **Fostering Collaboration:** Fostering collaboration between IT and the business to drive innovation and business outcomes.
- **Embracing Change:** Embracing change and being open to new ideas and approaches.

The role of IT is evolving from a cost center to a strategic business enabler in the AI-driven organization. By leveraging AI, developing key skills and competencies, and embracing change, IT leaders can drive business transformation and become strategic partners to the business. In the next section, we'll explore the future of AI and its implications for IT leaders.

Fostering Collaboration between IT and Business Units

Fostering collaboration between IT and business units is critical to ensuring that AI initiatives align with business objectives and deliver tangible business value. In this section, we'll explore the strategies for fostering collaboration, including establishing a shared vision, building trust, and creating cross-functional teams.

Establishing a Shared Vision

Establishing a shared vision involves aligning IT and business units around a common understanding of the organization's goals and objectives. This includes:

- **Business-IT Alignment:** Aligning IT strategies with business objectives.
- **Shared Goals:** Establishing shared goals and objectives for AI initiatives.
- **Clear Communication:** Ensuring clear communication between IT and business units.

Building Trust

Building trust involves establishing a foundation of trust between IT and business units, including:

- **Transparency:** Ensuring transparency in IT operations and decision-making.
- **Accountability:** Ensuring accountability for IT and business units.
- **Reliability:** Ensuring the reliability of IT services and solutions.

Creating Cross-Functional Teams

Creating cross-functional teams involves bringing together IT and business professionals to work collaboratively on AI initiatives. This includes:

- **Diverse Skill Sets:** Ensuring teams have diverse skill sets, including technical, business, and analytical skills.
- **Collaborative Culture:** Fostering a collaborative culture that encourages open communication and idea-sharing.
- **Clear Roles and Responsibilities:** Ensuring clear roles and responsibilities within cross-functional teams.

Key Considerations for Fostering Collaboration

Several key considerations must be taken into account when fostering collaboration between IT and business units, including:

- **Business Acumen:** Ensuring IT professionals have business acumen and understand the organization's goals and objectives.
- **Technical Expertise:** Ensuring that business professionals have technical expertise and understand the capabilities and limitations of AI.
- **Change Management:** Managing change and ensuring IT and business units are prepared to work collaboratively.
- **Continuous Feedback:** Encouraging continuous feedback and iteration to ensure that AI initiatives meet business needs.

Best Practices for Fostering Collaboration

Several best practices for fostering collaboration between IT and business units include:

- **Regular Meetings:** Holding regular meetings to ensure open communication and alignment.
- **Joint Goal Setting:** Setting joint goals and objectives for AI initiatives.
- **Cross-Functional Training:** It ensures IT and business professionals have the necessary skills and competencies.
- **Celebrating Successes:** Celebrating successes and recognizing the contributions of both IT and business units.

Fostering collaboration between IT and business units is critical to ensuring the success of AI initiatives. By establishing a shared vision, building trust, creating cross-functional teams, and considering key considerations and best practices, IT leaders can ensure that AI initiatives align with business objectives and deliver tangible business value. In the next section, we'll explore the future of AI and its implications for IT leaders.

Developing New Skills and Competencies for the AI Era

Developing new skills and competencies is critical for IT leaders to succeed in the AI era. In this section, we'll explore the latest skills and competencies required for IT leaders, including AI literacy, data science, and business acumen.

AI Literacy

AI literacy involves understanding the fundamentals of AI, including:

- **Machine Learning:** Understanding machine learning concepts, including supervised, unsupervised, and reinforcement learning.
- **Deep Learning:** Understanding deep learning concepts, including neural networks and natural language processing.
- **AI Applications:** Understanding the applications of AI, including computer vision, robotics, and natural language processing.

Data Science

Data science involves understanding the principles of data analysis, including:

- **Data Analysis:** Understanding data analysis techniques, including statistical analysis and data visualization.
- **Data Mining:** Understanding data mining techniques, including pattern recognition and predictive analytics.
- **Data Engineering:** Understanding data engineering principles, including architecture and governance.

Business Acumen

Business acumen involves understanding the organization's goals and objectives, including:

- **Business Strategy:** Understanding the organization's business strategy and objectives.
- **Industry Trends:** Understanding industry trends and how they impact the organization.
- **Financial Management:** Understanding financial management principles, including budgeting and cost management.

Key Skills for IT Leaders in the AI Era

Several key skills are required for IT leaders to succeed in the AI era, including:

- **Communication Skills:** Communicating effectively with both technical and non-technical stakeholders.
- **Collaboration Skills:** Collaborating effectively with cross-functional teams, including data scientists, business analysts, and developers.
- **Adaptability:** Adapting quickly to changing business needs and technological advancements.
- **Strategic Thinking:** Thinking strategically about how AI can drive business transformation.

Developing New Skills and Competencies

Developing new skills and competencies involves:

- **Training and Development:** Providing training and development opportunities for IT professionals.
- **Mentorship:** Providing mentorship opportunities for IT professionals to learn from experienced AI practitioners.
- **Cross-Functional Teams:** Creating cross-functional teams to combine diverse skill sets and expertise.
- **Continuous Learning:** Encouraging continuous learning and professional development.

Developing new skills and competencies is critical for IT leaders to succeed in the AI era. By understanding AI literacy, data science, business acumen, and key skills and developing them through training, mentorship, cross-functional teams, and continuous learning, IT leaders can ensure they can drive business transformation through AI. In the next section, we'll explore the future of AI and its implications for IT leaders.

Building a Culture of Innovation and Agility within IT

Building a culture of innovation and agility within IT is critical to ensuring that IT organizations respond quickly to changing business needs and leverage AI to drive business transformation. In this section, we'll explore the strategies for building a culture of innovation and agility, including fostering a culture of experimentation, embracing failure, and encouraging continuous learning.

Fostering a Culture of Experimentation

Fostering a culture of experimentation involves encouraging IT professionals to try new approaches and technologies, including:

- **Pilot Projects:** Conducting pilot projects to test new AI technologies and approaches.
- **Proof of Concepts:** Developing proof of concepts to demonstrate the potential of AI solutions.
- **Hackathons:** Hosting hackathons to encourage innovation and

collaboration.

Embracing Failure

Embracing failure involves recognizing that failure is a natural part of the innovation process and encouraging IT professionals to take calculated risks, including:

- **Risk Tolerance:** Encouraging a culture of risk tolerance and experimentation.
- **Lessons Learned:** Documenting lessons learned from failed experiments and applying them to future projects.
- **Celebrating Failure:** Celebrating failure as an opportunity to learn and grow.

Encouraging Continuous Learning

Encouraging continuous learning involves providing opportunities for IT professionals to develop new skills and stay up-to-date with the latest AI trends and technologies, including:

- **Training and Development:** Providing training and development opportunities for IT professionals.
- **Mentorship:** Providing mentorship opportunities for IT professionals to learn from experienced AI practitioners.

- **Industry Events:** Encouraging attendance at industry events and conferences to stay current with the latest AI trends and technologies.

Key Considerations for Building a Culture of Innovation and Agility

Several key considerations must be taken into account when building a culture of innovation and agility, including:

- **Leadership Buy-In:** Ensuring leadership buy-in and support for a culture of innovation and agility.
- **Change Management:** Managing change and ensuring IT professionals are prepared to work in a culture of innovation and agility.
- **Incentives:** Providing incentives for innovation and experimentation, such as recognition and rewards.
- **Feedback Mechanisms:** Establishing feedback mechanisms ensures that IT professionals can provide input and suggestions for improvement.

Best Practices for Building a Culture of Innovation and Agility

Several best practices for building a culture of innovation and agility include:

- **Empowerment:** Empowering IT professionals to make decisions and take ownership of projects.
- **Autonomy:** Providing autonomy to IT professionals to work on projects and initiatives that align with business objectives.
- **Collaboration:** Fostering collaboration between IT professionals and business stakeholders to ensure alignment with business objectives.
- **Recognition:** Recognizing and rewarding innovation and experimentation.

Building a culture of innovation and agility within IT is critical to ensuring that IT organizations respond quickly to changing business needs and leverage AI to drive business transformation. By fostering a culture of experimentation, embracing failure, encouraging continuous learning, and considering key considerations and best practices, IT leaders can ensure that their organizations are equipped to drive innovation and agility. In the next section, we'll explore the future of AI and its implications for IT leaders.

Summary and Key Points

In this chapter, we've explored the evolving role of IT in the AI-driven organization, including the transition from a cost center to a strategic business enabler, fostering collaboration between IT and business units, developing new skills and competencies for the AI era, and building a culture of innovation and agility within IT.

Summary

The chapter has covered:

1. **From Cost Center to Strategic Business Enabler:** The evolving role of IT from a cost center to a strategic business enabler in the AI-driven organization.
2. **Fostering Collaboration:** Fostering collaboration between IT and business units to ensure alignment with business objectives.
3. **Developing New Skills and Competencies:** Developing new skills and competencies, including AI literacy, data science, and business acumen, to succeed in the AI era.
4. **Building a Culture of Innovation and Agility:** Building a culture of innovation and agility within IT to drive business transformation.

Key Points

1. IT must evolve from a cost center to a strategic business enabler to drive business transformation.

2. Fostering collaboration between IT and business units is critical to ensuring alignment with business objectives.

3. Developing new skills and competencies, including AI literacy, data science, and business acumen, is essential for IT leaders to succeed in the AI era.

4. Building a culture of innovation and agility within IT is critical to driving business transformation and leveraging AI.

In the next chapter, we'll explore the future of AI and its implications for IT leaders, including the potential of AI to transform industries, the role of AI in digital transformation, and the skills and competencies required for AI-driven IT operations. This will provide a detailed understanding of how AI will continue to shape the future of IT operations and the implications for IT leaders.

IV

Part 4: The Future of IT

Chapter 9: Emerging Trends Shaping the Future of IT Infrastructure

Edge Computing and Its Implications for AI

As we navigate the ever-evolving landscape of IT infrastructure, it is imperative to acknowledge the transformative impact of emerging trends on the future of our industry. One such trend that has garnered significant attention in recent years is edge computing. In this chapter, we will delve into the concept of edge computing, its implications for AI, and how these advancements will shape the future of IT infrastructure.

What is Edge Computing?

Edge computing is a distributed computing paradigm that brings computation and data storage closer to the location where it is needed, reducing latency and improving real-time processing capabilities. This approach departs from the traditional cloud-centric model, where data is sent to a central server or cloud for processing. By processing data at the edge, organizations can significantly reduce the amount of data that needs to be transmitted, resulting in lower latency, improved security, and reduced bandwidth usage.

Key Drivers of Edge Computing

Several factors have contributed to the rise of edge computing:

- **IoT and Real-Time Data Processing:** The proliferation of IoT devices has led to an exponential increase in data generation. Edge computing enables real-time processing of this data, which is critical for applications such as autonomous vehicles, smart cities, and industrial automation.
- **5G Networks:** The advent of 5G networks has provided the necessary infrastructure for low-latency, high-bandwidth communication, making edge computing a viable solution for latency-sensitive applications.
- **Cloud Computing Limitations:** Cloud computing, while powerful, has limitations in terms of latency, security, and cost. Edge computing addresses these limitations by providing a more efficient and cost-effective solution.

Implications of Edge Computing for AI

The convergence of edge computing and AI has far-reaching implications for the future of IT infrastructure. AI models, particularly those leveraging machine learning and deep learning, are computationally intensive and require significant processing power. Edge computing offers several benefits for AI applications:

- **Real-Time Processing:** Edge computing enables real-time processing of data, which is critical for AI applications such as computer vision, natural language processing, and predictive analytics.
- **Reduced Latency:** By processing data closer to the source, edge computing reduces latency, making AI applications more responsive and effective.
- **Enhanced Security:** Edge computing reduces the amount of data transmitted to the cloud or central servers, minimizing the risk of data breaches and enhancing overall security.
- **Increased Efficiency:** Edge computing reduces the computational load on central servers, leading to increased efficiency and cost savings.

Edge AI Use Cases

Several use cases demonstrate the potential of edge AI:

- **Autonomous Vehicles:** Edge AI enables real-time sensor data processing, ensuring faster decision-making and improved safety.
- **Smart Cities:** Edge AI can monitor and manage city infrastructure, such as traffic management and energy consumption.
- **Industrial Automation:** Edge AI can optimize production processes, predict maintenance needs, and improve efficiency.

Challenges and Opportunities

While edge computing and AI offer significant benefits, there are challenges to be addressed:

- **Data Management:** Managing data at the edge requires new strategies and tools to ensure consistency, security, and integrity.
- **Infrastructure Complexity:** Edge computing infrastructure is more complex and distributed, requiring new management and orchestration tools.
- **Skills and Training:** IT professionals must develop new skills to design, deploy, and manage edge AI infrastructure.

Future Outlook

The future of IT infrastructure is poised to be shaped by the intersection of edge computing and AI. As edge computing continues to evolve, we can expect:

- **Increased Adoption:** Widespread adoption of edge computing across industries, driven by the need for real-time processing and reduced latency.
- **Advancements in AI:** Further advancements in AI, particularly in explainability, transparency, and edge-specific AI models.
- **New Business Models:** The emergence of new business models focused on edge AI services, such as edge AI as a service and edge AI-enabled IoT devices.

In conclusion, the future of IT infrastructure is being reshaped by the convergence of edge computing and AI. As IT leaders, we must understand these emerging trends and their implications, positioning our organizations for success in this rapidly evolving landscape. By embracing edge computing and AI, we can unlock new efficiencies, improve performance, and drive innovation in our industries.

Quantum Computing: The Next Frontier of IT Infrastructure?

Quantum computing is a rapidly emerging technology that has the potential to revolutionize the field of IT infrastructure. In this section, we'll explore the principles of quantum computing, its applications, and the implications for IT leaders.

Principles of Quantum Computing

Quantum computing is based on the principles of quantum mechanics, which differ fundamentally from classical computing. Key principles include:

- **Superposition:** Quantum bits (qubits) can exist in multiple states simultaneously, enabling parallel processing.
- **Entanglement:** Qubits can be connected, allowing for instantaneous communication.
- **Quantum Measurement:** Observing a qubit causes its state to collapse, introducing randomness.

Quantum Computing Applications

Quantum computing has the potential to solve complex problems in various domains, including:

- **Cryptography:** Quantum computers can break certain classical encryption algorithms, but they can also enable unbreakable quantum encryption.
- **Optimization:** Quantum computers can efficiently solve complex optimization problems, such as portfolio optimization and logistics.
- **Simulation:** Quantum computers can simulate complex systems, such as molecular interactions and materials science.

Implications for IT Infrastructure

The advent of quantum computing will have significant implications for IT infrastructure, including:

- **Quantum-Resistant Cryptography:** IT leaders must ensure that their cryptographic systems are quantum-resistant to prevent potential breaches.
- **Quantum-Enabled Optimization:** Quantum computers can optimize complex systems, such as supply chains and logistics, increasing efficiency and cost savings.
- **Quantum Simulation:** Quantum computers can simulate complex systems, enabling breakthroughs in medicine and materials sci-

ence.

Quantum Computing and AI

Quantum computing has the potential to enhance AI capabilities significantly.

- **Quantum AI:** Quantum computers can process vast amounts of data more efficiently, enabling faster and more accurate AI model training.
- **Quantum-Inspired AI:** Quantum-inspired AI algorithms can be run on classical computers, bridging classical and quantum computing.

Challenges and Opportunities

While quantum computing offers significant benefits, there are challenges to be addressed:

- **Quantum Noise and Error Correction:** Quantum computers are prone to errors due to quantum noise, requiring sophisticated error correction techniques.
- **Scalability:** Currently, quantum computers are small-scale and need to be scaled up to be practical for widespread use.
- **Talent and Training:** IT professionals must develop new skills to design, deploy, and manage quantum computing infrastructure.

Future Outlook

The future of IT infrastructure is poised to be shaped by the emergence of quantum computing. As quantum computing continues to evolve, we can expect:

- **Increased Adoption:** Widespread adoption of quantum computing across industries, driven by the need for faster processing and more efficient optimization.
- **Advancements in AI:** Further advancements in AI, particularly in quantum AI and quantum-inspired AI algorithms.
- **New Business Models:** The emergence of new business models focused on quantum computing services, such as quantum computing as a service and quantum-enabled AI solutions.

Quantum computing is the next frontier of IT infrastructure, offering significant potential for innovation and transformation. By understanding the principles, applications, and implications of quantum computing, IT leaders can position their organizations for success in this rapidly evolving landscape. By embracing quantum computing, we can unlock new efficiencies, improve performance, and drive innovation in our industries.

The Rise of Serverless Computing and Its Impact on AI Workloads

Serverless computing is a cloud computing model in which the cloud provider manages the infrastructure and dynamically allocates computing resources as needed. In this section, we'll explore the rise of serverless computing and its impact on AI workloads, including the benefits, challenges, and implications for IT leaders.

Benefits of Serverless Computing for AI Workloads

Serverless computing offers several benefits for AI workloads, including:

- **Scalability:** Serverless computing enables AI workloads to scale up or down dynamically, ensuring that resources are utilized efficiently.
- **Cost Savings:** Serverless computing reduces costs by only charging for the compute time consumed, making it a cost-effective solution for AI workloads.
- **Faster Deployment:** Serverless computing enables more rapid deployment of AI models, reducing the time and effort required for infrastructure setup and management.

Challenges of Serverless Computing for AI Workloads

While serverless computing offers several benefits, there are challenges to be addressed, including:

- **Cold Start:** Serverless functions may experience a "cold start" when first invoked, leading to increased latency.
- **Function Duration Limits:** Serverless functions have duration limits, which can impact the execution of long-running AI workloads.
- **Memory and Compute Constraints:** Serverless functions have memory and compute constraints, which can limit the complexity of AI models.

Implications for AI Workloads

The rise of serverless computing has significant implications for AI workloads, including:

- **AI Model Complexity:** Serverless computing enables the deployment of more complex AI models, which can lead to improved accuracy and performance.
- **Real-Time Processing:** Serverless computing enables real-time processing of AI workloads, critical for applications such as autonomous vehicles and smart cities.
- **Edge AI:** Serverless computing can deploy AI models at the edge, reducing latency and improving performance.

Key Considerations for IT Leaders

Several key considerations must be taken into account when adopting serverless computing for AI workloads, including:

- **Function Design:** Designing serverless functions to optimize performance and minimize cold starts.
- **Resource Utilization:** Ensuring that serverless functions utilize resources efficiently to minimize costs.
- **Security and Compliance:** Ensuring that serverless functions meet security and compliance requirements.

Best Practices for Serverless AI Workloads

Several best practices for serverless AI workloads include:

- **Function Optimization:** Optimizing serverless functions to minimize latency and improve performance.
- **Resource Provisioning:** Provisioning resources dynamically to ensure that they are utilized efficiently.
- **Monitoring and Logging:** Monitoring and logging serverless functions to ensure they operate as expected.

Future Outlook

The future of IT infrastructure is poised to be shaped by the rise of serverless computing and its impact on AI workloads. As serverless computing continues to evolve, we can expect:

- **Increased Adoption:** Widespread adoption of serverless computing for AI workloads, driven by the need for scalability, cost savings, and faster deployment.
- **Advancements in AI:** Further advancements in AI, particularly in areas like edge AI and real-time processing.
- **New Business Models:** The emergence of new business models focused on serverless AI services, such as serverless AI as a service and serverless AI-enabled edge computing.

Serverless computing is transforming the way AI workloads are deployed and managed. By understanding the benefits, challenges, and implications of serverless computing, IT leaders can position their organizations for success in this rapidly evolving landscape. By embracing serverless computing, we can unlock new efficiencies, improve performance, and drive innovation in our industries.

Blockchain Technology and Its Potential Applications in IT

Blockchain technology can transform various aspects of IT infrastructure, including security, data management, and supply chain management. In this section, we'll explore the principles of blockchain technology, its potential applications in IT, and its implications for IT leaders.

Principles of Blockchain Technology

Blockchain technology is based on a decentralized, distributed ledger that records transactions across a network of computers. Key principles include:

- **Decentralization:** Blockchain is a decentralized system, meaning that there is no central authority controlling the network.
- **Immutable Ledger:** The blockchain ledger is immutable, ensuring that once a transaction is recorded, it cannot be altered.
- **Consensus Mechanism:** A consensus mechanism ensures that all nodes on the network agree on the state of the blockchain.

Potential Applications in IT

Blockchain technology has several potential applications in IT, including:

- **Security:** Blockchain can enhance security by providing a secure and transparent way to store and manage sensitive data.
- **Data Management:** Blockchain can manage data decentralized and transparently, ensuring data integrity and provenance.
- **Supply Chain Management:** Blockchain can track and manage supply chains, ensuring transparency and accountability.

Implications for IT Leaders

The adoption of blockchain technology has significant implications for IT leaders, including:

- **New Business Models:** Blockchain enables new business models, such as decentralized applications and token-based economies.
- **Skills and Training:** IT professionals must develop new skills to design, deploy, and manage blockchain-based systems.
- **Infrastructure Upgrades:** Existing IT infrastructure may need to be upgraded to support blockchain-based applications.

Key Considerations for IT Leaders

Several key considerations must be taken into account when adopting blockchain technology, including:

- **Scalability:** Ensuring blockchain-based systems can scale to meet the organization's needs.
- **Interoperability:** Ensuring that blockchain-based systems can interoperate with existing systems and applications.
- **Regulatory Compliance:** Ensuring that blockchain-based systems meet regulatory requirements.

Best Practices for Blockchain Adoption

Several best practices for blockchain adoption include:

- **Pilot Projects:** Conducting pilot projects to test the feasibility and potential of blockchain technology.
- **Collaboration:** Collaborating with stakeholders to ensure that blockchain-based systems meet business needs.
- **Education and Training:** Educating and training IT professionals on blockchain technology and its applications.

Future Outlook

The future of IT infrastructure is poised to be shaped by adopting blockchain technology. As blockchain technology continues to evolve, we can expect:

- **Increased Adoption:** Widespread adoption of blockchain technology across industries, driven by the need for security, transparency, and accountability.
- **Advancements in AI:** Further advancements in AI, particularly in areas such as blockchain-based AI and AI-powered blockchain optimization.
- **New Business Models:** The emergence of new business models focused on blockchain-based services, such as blockchain as a service and blockchain-enabled supply chain management.

Blockchain technology has the potential to transform various aspects of IT infrastructure. By understanding the principles, applications, and implications of blockchain technology, IT leaders can position their organizations for success in this rapidly evolving landscape. By embracing blockchain technology, we can unlock new efficiencies, improve security, and drive innovation in our industries.

Summary and Key Points

In this chapter, we've explored emerging trends shaping the future of IT infrastructure, including edge computing, quantum computing, serverless computing, and blockchain technology.

Summary

The chapter has covered:

1. **Edge Computing:** The rise of edge computing and its implications for AI, including real-time processing, reduced latency, and enhanced security.
2. **Quantum Computing:** The principles of quantum computing, its applications, and the implications for IT leaders, including quantum-resistant cryptography, quantum-enabled optimization, and quantum simulation.
3. **Serverless Computing:** The rise of serverless computing and its impact on AI workloads, including scalability, cost savings, and faster deployment.
4. **Blockchain Technology:** The principles of blockchain technology, its potential applications in IT, and the implications for IT leaders, including security, data management, and supply chain management.

Key Points

1. Edge computing transforms how we process data, enabling real-time processing and reduced latency.

2. Quantum computing has the potential to revolutionize IT infrastructure, enabling faster processing and more efficient optimization.

3. Serverless computing transforms how we deploy and manage AI workloads, enabling scalability, cost savings, and faster deployment.

4. Blockchain technology can potentially transform various aspects of IT infrastructure, including security, data management, and supply chain management.

In the next chapter, we'll explore the future of AI and its implications for IT leaders, including the potential of AI to transform industries, the role of AI in digital transformation, and the skills and competencies required for AI-driven IT operations. This will provide a detailed understanding of how AI will continue to shape the future of IT operations and the implications for IT leaders.

Chapter 10: The Future of Work: How AI Will Reshape IT Staffing and Skills

The Impact of AI on IT Job Roles and Responsibilities

The advent of AI is transforming the IT landscape, and its impact on IT job roles and responsibilities cannot be overstated. In this section, we'll explore how AI is reshaping IT staffing and skills, including new roles, the evolution of existing roles, and the skills needed to thrive in an AI-driven IT environment.

Emergence of New Roles

AI is giving rise to new IT job roles, including:

- **AI/ML Engineer:** Responsible for designing, developing, and deploying AI and machine learning models.
- **Data Scientist:** Responsible for analyzing and interpreting complex data to inform business decisions.
- **AI Ethics Specialist:** Responsible for ensuring AI systems are

designed and deployed with ethical considerations.

Evolution of Existing Roles

Existing IT roles are evolving to incorporate AI, including:

- **IT Project Manager:** Now responsible for managing AI projects and ensuring their alignment with business objectives.
- **Network Administrator:** Now responsible for managing AI-powered network infrastructure and ensuring its security and reliability.
- **Help Desk Technician:** Now responsible for troubleshooting AI-powered systems and supporting end-users.

Skills Required to Thrive in an AI-Driven IT Environment

To thrive in an AI-driven IT environment, IT professionals will need to develop new skills, including:

- **AI Literacy:** Understanding the fundamentals of AI, including machine learning and deep learning.
- **Data Analysis:** Ability to analyze and interpret complex data to inform business decisions.
- **Cloud Computing:** Understanding cloud computing platforms and their role in supporting AI workloads.

- **Cybersecurity:** Understanding the security implications of AI and how to mitigate risks.

Upskilling and Reskilling

Upskilling and reskilling are critical to ensuring IT professionals remain relevant in an AI-driven IT environment. This includes:

- **Training and Development:** Providing training and development opportunities to enhance AI-related skills.
- **Mentorship:** Pairing IT professionals with experienced AI practitioners to learn from their expertise.
- **Certification Programs:** Encouraging IT professionals to pursue AI-related certifications to demonstrate their expertise.

Key Considerations for IT Leaders

Several key considerations must be taken into account when managing the impact of AI on IT job roles and responsibilities, including:

- **Change Management:** Managing change and ensuring IT professionals are prepared to work in an AI-driven environment.
- **Talent Acquisition:** Acquiring talent with AI-related skills to support business objectives.
- **Diversity and Inclusion:** Ensuring that AI-related skills are acces-

sible to a diverse range of IT professionals.

Best Practices for Managing AI-Driven IT Teams

Several best practices for managing AI-driven IT teams include:

- **Clear Communication:** Communicating the impact of AI on IT job roles and responsibilities.
- **Collaboration:** Fostering collaboration between IT professionals and AI practitioners to ensure successful AI adoption.
- **Continuous Learning:** Encouraging continuous learning and professional development ensures IT professionals remain relevant in an AI-driven environment.

Future Outlook

The future of IT staffing and skills is poised to be shaped by the impact of AI. As AI continues to evolve, we can expect the following:

- **Increased Demand for AI-Related Skills:** Widespread demand for AI-related skills across industries, driving the need for upskilling and reskilling.
- **New Business Models:** The emergence of new business models focused on AI-related services, such as AI consulting and AI training.
- **Diverse and Inclusive Workforce:** A diverse and inclusive work-

force with access to AI-related skills and training.

The impact of AI on IT job roles and responsibilities is significant. By understanding the emergence of new roles, the evolution of existing roles, and the skills required to thrive in an AI-driven IT environment, IT leaders can ensure their organizations are equipped to drive business transformation through AI. By embracing AI, we can unlock new efficiencies, improve performance, and drive innovation in our industries.

The Skills Gap in AI and How to Address It

The rapid adoption of AI across industries has created a significant skills gap, with many organizations struggling to find professionals with the necessary AI-related skills. In this section, we'll explore the skills gap in AI and how to address it, including the causes of the skills gap, the impact on organizations, and strategies for bridging the gap.

Causes of the Skills Gap

Several factors contribute to the skills gap in AI, including:

- **Lack of AI Education:** The lack of AI education and training programs, particularly at the undergraduate and graduate levels.
- **Rapid Advancements in AI:** The rapid pace of advancements in AI makes it challenging for professionals to keep up with the latest developments.

- **Limited AI Talent Pool:** The limited pool of professionals with AI-related skills, particularly in areas such as machine learning and deep learning.

Impact on Organizations

The skills gap in AI has significant implications for organizations, including:

- **Delayed AI Adoption:** The lack of AI-related skills can delay AI adoption, hindering business transformation and competitiveness.
- **Increased Costs:** The need to outsource AI work or hire expensive consultants can increase costs and reduce ROI.
- **Innovation Stagnation:** The lack of AI-related skills can stagnate innovation, making it challenging for organizations to stay ahead of the competition.

Strategies for Bridging the Gap

Several strategies can be employed to bridge the skills gap in AI, including:

- **Upskilling and Reskilling:** Upskilling and reskilling existing IT professionals to enhance AI-related skills.
- **Hiring AI Talent:** Hiring professionals with AI-related skills,

particularly in areas such as machine learning and deep learning.
- **Partnerships and Collaborations:** Forming partnerships and collaborations with AI vendors, startups, and academia to access AI expertise.
- **AI Education and Training:** Investing in AI education and training programs to develop a pipeline of AI talent.

Key Considerations for IT Leaders

Several key considerations must be taken into account when addressing the skills gap in AI, including:

- **Change Management:** Managing change and ensuring IT professionals are prepared to work in an AI-driven environment.
- **Talent Acquisition:** Acquiring talent with AI-related skills to support business objectives.
- **Diversity and Inclusion:** Ensuring that AI-related skills are accessible to a diverse range of IT professionals.

Best Practices for Addressing the Skills Gap

Several best practices for addressing the skills gap in AI include:

- **Developing an AI Strategy:** Develop an AI strategy that aligns with business objectives and identifies the necessary AI-related skills.

- **Creating an AI Talent Pipeline:** Creating a pipeline of AI talent through education and training programs.
- **Fostering a Culture of Innovation:** Fostering a culture of innovation that encourages experimentation and learning.

Future Outlook

The future of IT staffing and skills is poised to be shaped by the skills gap in AI. As AI continues to evolve, we can expect the following:

- **Increased Demand for AI-Related Skills:** Widespread demand for AI-related skills across industries, driving the need for upskilling and reskilling.
- **New Business Models:** The emergence of new business models focused on AI-related services, such as AI consulting and AI training.
- **Diverse and Inclusive Workforce:** A diverse and inclusive workforce with access to AI-related skills and training.

The skills gap in AI is a significant challenge facing organizations today. By understanding the causes of the skills gap, the impact on organizations, and strategies for bridging it, IT leaders can ensure their organizations are equipped to drive business transformation through AI. By addressing the skills gap, we can unlock new efficiencies, improve performance, and drive innovation in our industries.

Upskilling and Reskilling the IT Workforce for the AI Era

Upskilling and reskilling the IT workforce is critical to ensuring organizations have the necessary skills to drive business transformation through AI. In this section, we'll explore the strategies for upskilling and reskilling the IT workforce, including identifying AI-related skills, developing training programs, and creating a culture of continuous learning.

Identifying AI-Related Skills

Identifying AI-related skills is the first step in upskilling and reskilling the IT workforce. This includes:

- **AI Literacy:** Understanding the fundamentals of AI, including machine learning and deep learning.
- **Data Analysis:** Ability to analyze and interpret complex data to inform business decisions.
- **Cloud Computing:** Understanding cloud computing platforms and their role in supporting AI workloads.
- **Cybersecurity:** Understanding the security implications of AI and how to mitigate risks.

Developing Training Programs

Developing training programs is essential to upskilling and reskilling the IT workforce. This includes:

- **AI-Related Courses:** Develop courses focusing on AI-related skills, such as machine learning, deep learning, and natural language processing.
- **Hands-On Training:** Providing hands-on training opportunities ensures IT professionals can apply AI-related skills in real-world scenarios.
- **Mentorship:** Pairing IT professionals with experienced AI practitioners to learn from their expertise.
- **Certification Programs:** Encouraging IT professionals to pursue AI-related certifications to demonstrate their expertise.

Creating a Culture of Continuous Learning

Creating a culture of continuous learning is critical to ensuring that the IT workforce remains relevant in an AI-driven environment. This includes:

- **Encouraging Experimentation:** Encouraging IT professionals to experiment with AI technologies and develop new skills.
- **Providing Resources:** Providing resources, such as online courses and training materials, to support continuous learning.
- **Recognizing and Rewarding:** Recognizing and rewarding IT pro-

fessionals who develop and apply new AI-related skills to drive business value.
- **Fostering Collaboration:** Fostering collaboration between IT professionals and AI practitioners to ensure knowledge sharing and skill development.

Key Considerations for IT Leaders

Several key considerations must be taken into account when upskilling and reskilling the IT workforce, including:

- **Change Management:** Managing change and ensuring IT professionals are prepared to work in an AI-driven environment.
- **Talent Acquisition:** Acquiring talent with AI-related skills to support business objectives.
- **Diversity and Inclusion:** Ensuring that AI-related skills are accessible to a diverse range of IT professionals.

Best Practices for Upskilling and Reskilling

Several best practices for upskilling and reskilling the IT workforce include:

- **Developing a Skills Framework:** Develop a skills framework that outlines the necessary AI-related skills for each role.

- **Creating a Learning Path:** It outlines the training and development opportunities available to IT professionals.
- **Encouraging Knowledge Sharing:** Encouraging knowledge sharing between IT professionals and AI practitioners to ensure that skills are transferred effectively.
- **Monitoring Progress:** Monitoring progress and adjusting training programs to ensure that IT professionals are developing the necessary AI-related skills.

Future Outlook

The future of IT staffing and skills is poised to be shaped by the need for upskilling and reskilling the IT workforce. As AI continues to evolve, we can expect the following:

- **Increased Demand for AI-Related Skills:** Widespread demand for AI-related skills across industries, driving the need for upskilling and reskilling.
- **New Business Models:** The emergence of new business models focused on AI-related services, such as AI consulting and AI training.
- **Diverse and Inclusive Workforce:** A diverse and inclusive workforce with access to AI-related skills and training.

Upskilling and reskilling the IT workforce is critical to ensuring organizations have the necessary skills to drive business transformation through AI. By identifying AI-related skills, developing training programs, and creating a culture of continuous learning, IT leaders can ensure their organizations are equipped to thrive in an AI-driven environment. By embracing upskilling and reskilling, we can unlock new efficiencies, improve performance, and drive innovation in our industries.

The Importance of Continuous Learning and Professional Development

Continuous learning and professional development are critical to ensuring that IT professionals remain relevant in an AI-driven environment. In this section, we'll explore the importance of continuous learning and professional development, including the benefits, challenges, and strategies for implementing a culture of continuous learning.

Benefits of Continuous Learning

Continuous learning and professional development offer several benefits, including:

- **Staying Relevant:** Ensuring that IT professionals stay relevant in an AI-driven environment.
- **Enhanced Skills:** Enhancing AI-related skills, such as machine learning, deep learning, and natural language processing.
- **Improved Performance:** Improving performance and driving business value through AI adoption.
- **Competitive Advantage:** Gaining a competitive advantage by staying ahead of the curve in AI adoption.

Challenges of Continuous Learning

Several challenges must be addressed when implementing a culture of continuous learning, including:

- **Time Constraints:** Finding time for continuous learning and professional development amidst busy schedules.
- **Cost:** The cost of training and development programs, particularly for AI-related skills.
- **Access to Resources:** Ensuring access to resources, such as online courses and training materials, to support continuous learning.

Strategies for Implementing a Culture of Continuous Learning

Several strategies can be employed to implement a culture of continuous learning, including:

- **Mandatory Training:** Making training and development mandatory for IT professionals.
- **Flexible Learning Options:** Providing flexible learning options, such as online courses and self-paced training, to accommodate different learning styles.
- **Mentorship:** Pairing IT professionals with experienced AI practitioners to learn from their expertise.
- **Recognition and Rewards:** Recognizing and rewarding IT professionals who develop and apply new AI-related skills to drive

business value.

Key Considerations for IT Leaders

Several key considerations must be taken into account when implementing a culture of continuous learning, including:

- **Change Management:** Managing change and ensuring IT professionals are prepared to work in an AI-driven environment.
- **Talent Acquisition:** Acquiring talent with AI-related skills to support business objectives.
- **Diversity and Inclusion:** Ensuring that AI-related skills are accessible to a diverse range of IT professionals.

Best Practices for Continuous Learning

Several best practices for continuous learning include:

- **Developing a Learning Strategy:** Develop a learning strategy that outlines the necessary AI-related skills for each role.
- **Creating a Learning Path:** It outlines the training and development opportunities available to IT professionals.
- **Encouraging Knowledge Sharing:** Encouraging knowledge sharing between IT professionals and AI practitioners to ensure that skills are transferred effectively.

- **Monitoring Progress:** Monitoring progress and adjusting training programs to ensure that IT professionals are developing the necessary AI-related skills.

Future Outlook

The future of IT staffing and skills is poised to be shaped by the importance of continuous learning and professional development. As AI continues to evolve, we can expect the following:

- **Increased Demand for AI-Related Skills:** Widespread demand for AI-related skills across industries, driving the need for continuous learning and professional development.
- **New Business Models:** The emergence of new business models focused on AI-related services, such as AI consulting and AI training.
- **Diverse and Inclusive Workforce:** A diverse and inclusive workforce with access to AI-related skills and training.

Continuous learning and professional development are critical to ensuring that IT professionals remain relevant in an AI-driven environment. By understanding the benefits, challenges, and strategies for implementing a culture of continuous learning, IT leaders can ensure their organizations are equipped to drive business transformation through AI. By embracing continuous learning, we can unlock new efficiencies, improve performance, and drive innovation in our industries.

Summary and Key Points

In this chapter, we've explored the future of work and how AI will reshape IT staffing and skills, including the impact of AI on IT job roles and responsibilities, the skills gap in AI, upskilling and reskilling the IT workforce, and the importance of continuous learning and professional development.

Summary

The chapter has covered:

1. **The Impact of AI on IT Job Roles and Responsibilities:** The emergence of new roles, the evolution of existing roles, and the skills required to thrive in an AI-driven IT environment.
2. **The Skills Gap in AI:** The causes of the skills gap, the impact on organizations, and strategies for bridging the gap.
3. **Upskilling and Reskilling the IT Workforce:** Identifying AI-related skills, developing training programs, and creating a culture of continuous learning.
4. **The Importance of Continuous Learning and Professional Development:** The benefits, challenges, and strategies for implementing a culture of continuous learning.

Key Points

1. AI is transforming IT job roles and responsibilities, requiring new skills and competencies.

2. The skills gap in AI is a significant challenge facing organizations, requiring upskilling and reskilling of the IT workforce.

3. Upskilling and reskilling the IT workforce is critical to ensuring organizations have the necessary skills to drive business transformation through AI.

4. Continuous learning and professional development ensure that IT professionals remain relevant in an AI-driven environment.

In the next chapter, we'll explore the future of AI and its implications for IT leaders, including the potential of AI to transform industries, the role of AI in digital transformation, and the skills and competencies required for AI-driven IT operations. This will provide a detailed understanding of how AI will continue to shape the future of IT operations and the implications for IT leaders.

Chapter 11: Building a Roadmap for AI-Driven IT Transformation

Key Steps for Developing an AI Strategy for IT

Developing an AI strategy for IT is critical to ensuring that organizations leverage AI effectively to drive business transformation. In this section, we'll explore the key steps for developing an AI strategy for IT, including assessing readiness, defining AI goals, identifying AI opportunities, and creating an AI roadmap.

Assessing Readiness

Assessing readiness involves evaluating the organization's current state and identifying areas that need improvement, including:

- **Current IT Infrastructure:** Evaluating the current IT infrastructure and identifying areas that need upgrading or modernization.
- **Data Readiness:** Evaluating the quality and readiness of data for AI adoption.

- **Skills and Competencies:** Evaluating the skills and competencies of the IT workforce and identifying areas that need upskilling or reskilling.

Defining AI Goals

Defining AI goals involves identifying the business objectives that AI will support, including:

- **Business Objectives:** Identifying the business objectives AI will support, such as cost reduction, improved customer experience, or increased revenue.
- **Key Performance Indicators (KPIs):** Defining KPIs to measure the success of AI initiatives.
- **AI Vision:** Developing a clear AI vision that aligns with business objectives.

Identifying AI Opportunities

Identifying AI opportunities involves identifying areas where AI can add value, including:

- **Process Automation:** Identifying processes that can be automated using AI.
- **Predictive Analytics:** Identifying areas where predictive analytics

can drive business value.
- **Customer Experience:** Identifying areas where AI can improve customer experience.

Creating an AI Roadmap

Creating an AI roadmap involves outlining the steps necessary to achieve AI goals, including:

- **Short-Term Goals:** Identifying short-term goals and objectives that can be achieved within 6-12 months.
- **Long-Term Goals:** Identifying long-term goals and objectives that can be achieved within 1-3 years.
- **Key Initiatives:** Identifying key initiatives supporting AI adoption, such as upskilling and reskilling the IT workforce.

Key Considerations for IT Leaders

Several key considerations must be taken into account when developing an AI strategy for IT, including:

- **Change Management:** Managing change and ensuring the organization is prepared to work in an AI-driven environment.
- **Talent Acquisition:** Acquiring talent with AI-related skills to support business objectives.

- **Diversity and Inclusion:** Ensuring that AI-related skills are accessible to a diverse range of IT professionals.

Best Practices for Developing an AI Strategy

Several best practices for developing an AI strategy include:

- ~~Collaboration:~~ Collaborating with stakeholders ensures the AI strategy aligns with business objectives.
- **Flexibility:** Ensuring the AI strategy is flexible and adaptable to changing business needs.
- **Continuous Monitoring:** Continuously monitoring the AI strategy and adjusting as needed to ensure alignment with business objectives.

Future Outlook

The future of IT is poised to be shaped by the development of AI strategies that align with business objectives. As AI continues to evolve, we can expect the following:

- **Increased Adoption:** Widespread adoption of AI across industries, driving the need for effective AI strategies.
- **New Business Models:** The emergence of new business models focused on AI-related services, such as AI consulting and AI training.

- **Diverse and Inclusive Workforce:** A diverse and inclusive workforce with access to AI-related skills and training.

Developing an AI strategy for IT is critical to ensuring that organizations leverage AI effectively to drive business transformation. By assessing readiness, defining AI goals, identifying AI opportunities, and creating an AI roadmap, IT leaders can ensure their organizations are equipped to thrive in an AI-driven environment. By embracing AI, we can unlock new efficiencies, improve performance, and drive innovation in our industries.

Assessing Organizational Readiness for AI Adoption

Assessing organizational readiness for AI adoption is a critical step in developing an AI strategy for IT. In this section, we'll explore the key factors to consider when assessing organizational readiness, including IT infrastructure, data readiness, skills and competencies, and change management.

IT Infrastructure

Assessing IT infrastructure involves evaluating the current state of the organization's IT infrastructure and identifying areas that need upgrading or modernization, including:

- **Hardware and Software:** Evaluating the current hardware and

software capabilities and identifying areas that need upgrading or modernization.
- **Network and Connectivity:** Evaluating the current network and connectivity capabilities and identifying areas that need upgrading or modernization.
- **Cloud Readiness:** Evaluating the organization's cloud readiness and identifying areas that need upgrading or modernization.

Data Readiness

Assessing data readiness involves evaluating the quality and readiness of the organization's data for AI adoption, including:

- **Data Quality:** Evaluating the quality of the organization's data and identifying areas that need improvement.
- **Data Integration:** Evaluating data integration across different systems and identifying areas that need improvement.
- **Data Governance:** Evaluating the organization's data governance policies and identifying areas that need improvement.

Skills and Competencies

Assessing skills and competencies involves evaluating the skills and competencies of the IT workforce and identifying areas that need upskilling or reskilling, including:

- **AI Literacy:** Evaluating the AI literacy of the IT workforce and identifying areas that need improvement.
- **Data Analysis:** Evaluating the data analysis skills of the IT workforce and identifying areas that need improvement.
- **Cloud Computing:** Evaluating the cloud computing skills of the IT workforce and identifying areas that need improvement.

Change Management

Assessing change management involves evaluating the organization's ability to manage change and identifying areas that need improvement, including:

- **Change Culture:** Evaluating the organization's culture and identifying areas that need improvement to support AI adoption.
- **Communication:** Evaluating the organization's communication strategies and identifying areas that need improvement to support AI adoption.
- **Training and Development:** Evaluating the organization's training and development programs and identifying areas that need improvement to support AI adoption.

Key Considerations for IT Leaders

Several key considerations must be taken into account when assessing organizational readiness for AI adoption, including:

- **Business Objectives:** Ensuring that AI adoption aligns with business objectives.
- **Talent Acquisition:** Acquiring talent with AI-related skills to support business objectives.
- **Diversity and Inclusion:** Ensuring that AI-related skills are accessible to a diverse range of IT professionals.

Best Practices for Assessing Organizational Readiness

Several best practices for assessing organizational readiness include:

- **Conducting a Gap Analysis:** Conducting a gap analysis to identify areas that need improvement.
- **Developing a Maturity Model:** Develop a maturity model to evaluate the organization's readiness for AI adoption.
- **Engaging Stakeholders:** To ensure that the assessment is comprehensive and accurate.

Future Outlook

The future of IT is poised to be shaped by the assessment of organizational readiness for AI adoption. As AI continues to evolve, we can expect the following:

- **Increased Adoption:** Widespread adoption of AI across industries, driving the need for effective assessments of organizational readiness.
- **New Business Models:** The emergence of new business models focused on AI-related services, such as AI consulting and AI training.
- **Diverse and Inclusive Workforce:** A diverse and inclusive workforce with access to AI-related skills and training.

Assessing organizational readiness for AI adoption is critical to ensuring that organizations can effectively leverage AI. By evaluating IT infrastructure, data readiness, skills and competencies, and change management, IT leaders can ensure their organizations are prepared to thrive in an AI-driven environment. By embracing AI, we can unlock new efficiencies, improve performance, and drive innovation in our industries.

Building a Business Case for AI Investments in IT

Building a business case for AI investments in IT is critical to securing funding and support for AI initiatives. In this section, we'll explore the key steps for building a business case, including identifying business objectives, quantifying benefits, and developing a financial model.

Identifying Business Objectives

Identifying business objectives involves aligning AI initiatives with business goals, including:

- **Cost Reduction:** Identifying areas where AI can reduce costs, such as automation of manual processes.
- **Revenue Growth:** Identifying areas where AI can drive revenue growth, such as improved customer experience.
- **Competitive Advantage:** Identifying areas where AI can provide a competitive advantage, such as predictive analytics.

Quantifying Benefits

Quantifying benefits involves estimating the financial impact of AI initiatives, including:

- **Cost Savings:** Estimating the cost savings resulting from AI adoption.
- **Revenue Growth:** Estimating the revenue growth resulting from AI adoption.
- **Productivity Gains:** Estimating the productivity gains resulting from AI adoption.

Developing a Financial Model

Developing a financial model involves creating a detailed financial plan for AI initiatives, including:

- **Cost Estimates:** Estimating the costs associated with AI adoption, including hardware, software, and personnel costs.
- **Return on Investment (ROI) Analysis:** Conducting an ROI analysis to determine the financial return on AI investments.
- **Break-Even Analysis:** Conducting a break-even analysis to determine when AI investments will pay off.

Key Considerations for IT Leaders

Several key considerations must be taken into account when building a business case for AI investments in IT, including:

- **Business Alignment:** Ensuring that AI initiatives align with business objectives.
- **Financial Transparency:** Ensuring financial transparency and accountability for AI investments.
- **Risk Management:** Managing risks associated with AI adoption, such as data privacy and security risks.

Best Practices for Building a Business Case

Several best practices for building a business case include:

- **Collaboration:** Collaborating with stakeholders to ensure that the business case aligns with business objectives.
- **Data-Driven Approach:** Using a data-driven approach to quantify benefits and estimate costs.
- **Flexibility:** Ensuring the business case is flexible and adaptable to changing business needs.

Future Outlook

The future of IT is poised to be shaped by the development of business cases for AI investments. As AI continues to evolve, we can expect the following:

- **Increased Adoption:** Widespread adoption of AI across industries, driving the need for effective business cases.
- **New Business Models:** The emergence of new business models focused on AI-related services, such as AI consulting and AI training.
- **Diverse and Inclusive Workforce:** A diverse and inclusive workforce with access to AI-related skills and training.

Building a business case for AI investments in IT is critical to securing funding and support for AI initiatives. By identifying business objectives, quantifying benefits, and developing a financial model, IT leaders can ensure their organizations are equipped to leverage AI effectively. By embracing AI, we can unlock new efficiencies, improve performance, and drive innovation in our industries.

Measuring the Success of AI Initiatives in IT

Measuring the success of AI initiatives in IT is critical to ensuring that AI adoption aligns with business objectives and delivers tangible value. In this section, we'll explore the key metrics for measuring the success of AI initiatives, including ROI analysis, KPIs, and metrics for AI adoption.

ROI Analysis

Conducting an ROI analysis involves evaluating the financial return on AI investments, including:

- **Cost Savings:** Measuring the cost savings resulting from AI adoption.
- **Revenue Growth:** Measuring the revenue growth resulting from AI adoption.
- **Productivity Gains:** Measuring the productivity gains resulting from AI adoption.

Key Performance Indicators (KPIs)

Establishing KPIs involves identifying metrics that measure the success of AI initiatives, including:

- **Automation Rate:** Measuring the percentage of processes automated using AI.
- **Accuracy Improvement:** Measuring the improvement in accuracy resulting from AI adoption.
- **Response Time Reduction:** Measuring the reduction in response time resulting from AI adoption.

Metrics for AI Adoption

Several metrics can be used to measure the success of AI adoption, including:

- **AI Model Accuracy:** Measuring the accuracy of AI models in predicting outcomes or classifying data.
- **Data Quality Improvement:** Measuring the improvement in data quality resulting from AI adoption.
- **User Adoption Rate:** Measuring the user adoption rate of AI-powered systems and applications.

CHAPTER 11: BUILDING A ROADMAP FOR AI-DRIVEN IT...

Key Considerations for IT Leaders

Several key considerations must be taken into account when measuring the success of AI initiatives, including:

- **Business Alignment:** Ensuring that metrics align with business objectives.
- **Data Quality:** Ensuring that data used to measure success is accurate and reliable.
- **Continuous Monitoring:** Continuously monitoring metrics to ensure that AI initiatives are on track to deliver expected outcomes.

Best Practices for Measuring Success

Several best practices for measuring the success of AI initiatives include:

- **Establishing Baselines:** Establishing baselines to measure the impact of AI adoption.
- **Defining Success Criteria:** Defining success criteria ensures metrics align with business objectives.
- **Regular Review:** Regularly reviewing metrics to ensure that AI initiatives are on track to deliver expected outcomes.

Future Outlook

The future of IT is poised to be shaped by the measurement of AI success. As AI continues to evolve, we can expect the following:

- **Increased Adoption:** Widespread adoption of AI across industries, driving the need for effective metrics to measure success.
- **New Business Models:** The emergence of new business models focused on AI-related services, such as AI consulting and AI training.
- **Diverse and Inclusive Workforce:** A diverse and inclusive workforce with access to AI-related skills and training.

Measuring the success of AI initiatives in IT is critical to ensuring that AI adoption aligns with business objectives and delivers tangible value. By conducting ROI analysis, establishing KPIs, and using metrics for AI adoption, IT leaders can ensure their organizations are equipped to leverage AI effectively. By embracing AI, we can unlock new efficiencies, improve performance, and drive innovation in our industries.

Summary and Key Points

In this chapter, we've explored building a roadmap for AI-driven IT transformation, including key steps for developing an AI strategy for IT, assessing organizational readiness for AI adoption, building a business case for AI investments in IT, and measuring the success of AI initiatives in IT.

Summary

The chapter has covered:

1. **Key Steps for Developing an AI Strategy for IT:** Assessing readiness, defining AI goals, identifying AI opportunities, and creating an AI roadmap.
2. **Assessing Organizational Readiness for AI Adoption:** Evaluating IT infrastructure, data readiness, skills and competencies, and change management.
3. **Building a Business Case for AI Investments in IT:** Identifying business objectives, quantifying benefits, and developing a financial model.
4. **Measuring the Success of AI Initiatives in IT:** Conducting ROI analysis, establishing KPIs, and using metrics for AI adoption.

Key Points

1. Developing an AI strategy for IT is critical to ensuring that organizations leverage AI effectively to drive business transformation.

2. Assessing organizational readiness for AI adoption is essential to identifying areas that need improvement.

3. Building a business case for AI investments in IT is necessary to secure funding and support for AI initiatives.

4. Measuring the success of AI initiatives in IT is critical to ensuring that AI adoption aligns with business objectives and delivers tangible value.

Conclusion

In this book, we've embarked on a journey to explore the transformative power of AI in IT infrastructure. We've delved into the current state of AI in IT, the benefits and challenges of AI adoption, and the strategies for aligning IT with business transformation. We've also examined the emerging trends shaping the future of IT infrastructure, including edge computing, quantum computing, serverless computing, and blockchain technology. Finally, we've discussed the future of work and how AI will reshape IT staffing and skills and build a roadmap for AI-driven IT transformation.

Summary of Key Takeaways

1. **AI is transforming IT infrastructure:** AI is revolutionizing how we manage and maintain IT infrastructure, enabling automation, efficiency, and innovation.

2. **Benefits of AI adoption:** AI adoption can lead to cost savings, improved performance, and enhanced customer experience.

3. **Challenges of AI adoption:** AI adoption also presents challenges,

including data quality issues, talent acquisition, and change management.

4. Aligning IT with business transformation: AI can help align IT with business objectives, enabling digital transformation and driving business value.

5. Emerging trends: Emerging trends like edge computing, quantum computing, serverless computing, and blockchain technology will continue to shape the future of IT infrastructure.

6. Future of work: AI will reshape IT staffing and skills, requiring upskilling and reskilling of the IT workforce.

7. Roadmap for AI-driven IT transformation: Developing an AI strategy, assessing organizational readiness, building a business case, and measuring success are critical steps in building a roadmap for AI-driven IT transformation.

Call to Action

As we conclude this book, we urge IT leaders to take action and embark on their AI-driven IT transformation journey. AI is shaping the future of IT, and it's essential to stay ahead of the curve. Here are some key actions to take:

1. Start small: Begin with pilot projects or proof of concepts to test AI capabilities and build momentum.

2. Upskill and reskill: Invest in upskilling and reskilling the IT workforce to ensure they have the necessary AI-related skills.

3. Develop an AI strategy: Create a clear AI strategy that aligns with business objectives and identifies areas for AI adoption.

4. Assess organizational readiness: Evaluate the organization's readiness for AI adoption and identify improvement areas.

5. Build a business case: Develop a compelling business case for AI investments, quantifying benefits and estimating costs.

6. Measure success: Establish metrics to measure the success of AI initiatives and ensure they align with business objectives.

By embracing AI and taking these actions, IT leaders can unlock new efficiencies, improve performance, and drive innovation in their organizations. The future of IT is bright, and AI is leading the way.

About the Author

Edgardo Fernandez Climent, an accomplished IT leader with over two decades of experience, has significantly contributed to infrastructure, networks, and cybersecurity. His exceptional leadership skills and strategic vision have positioned him as a prominent figure in the industry. After graduating with honors in Computer Information Systems, Edgardo pursued an MBA and a Master's in Management Information Systems, further enhancing his expertise. He also holds several industry certifications, such as PMP, ITIL4, and Security+, demonstrating his commitment to professional development and staying at the forefront of industry standards.

Throughout his career, Edgardo has consistently demonstrated his ability to lead organizations through complex technological transformations. His deep understanding of emerging technologies and industry trends has enabled him to develop and implement innovative strategies that drive business growth and ensure technological resilience. Edgardo's leadership in navigating the ever-changing landscape of cybersecurity has been instrumental in safeguarding organizations against the evolving threats of the digital world.

As a visionary leader, Edgardo is known for his ability to inspire and motivate teams to achieve excellence. He fosters a culture of continuous learning and encourages his team members to embrace new technologies and develop their skills. Edgardo's commitment to mentoring and developing the next generation of IT leaders has profoundly impacted the industry as he shares his knowledge and experiences to empower others to succeed.

Edgardo's leadership style is characterized by his ability to build strong relationships, promote collaboration, and drive results. He has a proven track record of successfully leading cross-functional teams and aligning IT initiatives with business objectives. His strategic thinking, combined with his technical expertise, has enabled him to develop and execute transformative initiatives that have delivered significant value to the organizations he has served.

Today, as a highly sought-after consultant in the IT industry, Edgardo continues to be at the forefront of shaping the technological landscape. His leadership and expertise are highly valued by organizations seeking to drive innovation, optimize their IT infrastructure, and strengthen their cybersecurity posture. Edgardo's journey is a testament to the power of visionary leadership, continuous learning, and a relentless pursuit of excellence in the ever-evolving field of information technology.

You can connect with me on:
- https://fernandezcliment.com
- https://twitter.com/efernandezclime
- https://www.facebook.com/edgardo.fernandez.climent
- https://amazon.com/author/efernandezcliment

Subscribe to my newsletter:
- https://fernandezcliment.com/join-our-mail-list

Also by Edgardo Fernandez Climent

AIOps: Revolutionizing IT Operations with Artificial Intelligence

"AIOps: Revolutionizing IT Operations with Artificial Intelligence" is a must-read for IT professionals looking to leverage the transformative power of AI and machine learning in IT operations. This comprehensive guide demystifies the concepts, technologies, and best practices behind AIOps, enabling readers to implement intelligent automation, predictive analytics, and data-driven decision-making in their organizations.

The book begins by introducing the fundamental principles and components of AIOps, including data ingestion, anomaly detection, root cause analysis, and automated remediation. It then delves into real-world use cases and applications, showcasing how AIOps can revolutionize incident management, performance optimization, capacity planning, and user experience.

Readers will learn how to build and train AI models, integrate AIOps with existing IT processes and tools, and establish governance frameworks for responsible and ethical AI deployment. The book also explores the organizational and cultural aspects of AIOps adoption, providing strategies for change management, skill development, and continuous improvement.

Through practical examples, case studies, and expert insights, this book empowers IT professionals to harness the full potential of AIOps and drive digital transformation in their organizations. Whether you are an IT manager, system administrator, or data scientist, this book provides the knowledge and guidance needed to succeed in AI-driven IT operations.

AI-Powered Cybersecurity: The Promise and Perils of Generative AI

"AI-Powered Cybersecurity: The Promise and Perils of Generative AI" is a must-read for IT professionals seeking to understand and harness the power of GenAI in cybersecurity. This book explores GenAI's applications, benefits, and challenges in various cybersecurity domains, including threat detection, incident response, vulnerability management, and more.

The author, a practitioner with extensive experience in cybersecurity, AI, and GenAI, provides a balanced perspective on the potential of these technologies while also addressing critical concerns such as bias, explainability, and accountability. Through real-world case studies and practical insights, readers will learn how to effectively implement GenAI in their cybersecurity strategies and navigate AI-powered security's ethical and societal implications.

Whether you are a seasoned cybersecurity professional or an IT leader looking to stay ahead of the curve, this book will equip you with the knowledge and tools to make informed decisions about GenAI in your organization. Join the forefront of the cybersecurity revolution and discover how Generative AI is shaping the future of digital defense.

GenAI and Project Management: New Roles, New Opportunities: The Essential Handbook for Project Managers in the GenAI Era

"GenAI and Project Management: New Roles, New Opportunities" is the essential handbook for project managers navigating the AI revolution.

Based on extensive real-world experience, this comprehensive guide explores how Generative AI reshapes project management practices across industries. From AI-driven risk assessment to automated resource allocation, learn how to leverage cutting-edge technologies to enhance project outcomes.

Discover strategies for upskilling your team, ethically implementing AI tools, and positioning yourself as a strategic leader in the AI-augmented workplace.

With practical case studies, actionable insights, and a toolkit of AI integration templates, this book equips you to thrive in the evolving landscape of project management.

Whether you're a seasoned PMP or an aspiring project leader, this invaluable resource will help unlock AI's transformative potential in your projects and career.

Al-Powered Agile
Edgardo Fernandez Climent

AI-Powered Agile: Revolutionizing Project Management with Artificial Intelligence

Discover how the transformative power of artificial intelligence (AI) is revolutionizing agile project management with "AI-Powered Agile: Revolutionizing Project Management with AI." This groundbreaking book explores the intersection of AI and agile, revealing how AI technologies can be leveraged to enhance and optimize every aspect of the agile lifecycle.

In this book, you'll learn how to:
 - Harness AI-powered insights and recommendations to streamline sprint planning and backlog management
 - Utilize AI-driven virtual assistants and sentiment analysis to optimize team collaboration and communication
 - Implement adaptive project management practices using machine learning and predictive analytics
 - Mitigate risks and improve decision-making with AI-powered forecasting and scenario planning
 - Foster a culture of continuous learning and experimentation with AI in agile teams

The author provides a comprehensive framework for integrating AI into agile practices through in-depth research, real-world case studies, and practical insights. They address critical challenges and considerations, such as data quality, ethical implications, and cultural adoption, ensuring that you have a holistic understanding of AI's impact on agile project management.

Whether you are an agile practitioner, project manager, or business leader, "AI-powered Agile" equips you with the knowledge and tools to leverage AI's power in your agile projects. The book offers a compelling vision of how humans and artificial intelligence can work together to achieve exceptional results and drive organizational success.

Key features of the book include:

- Comprehensive coverage of AI technologies and their applications in agile project management

- Practical templates and tools for implementing AI-powered agile practices

- Real-world case studies and examples from industry leaders

- Strategies for overcoming challenges and fostering a culture of AI adoption

- Future trends and opportunities for AI in agile project management

"AI-Powered Agile" is not just a book but a roadmap for navigating the future of project management in an increasingly AI-driven world. It is an essential guide for anyone looking to stay ahead of the curve and unlock the full potential of AI in their agile practices.

Take advantage of this transformative journey that will reshape how you think about and execute agile project management in the age of AI. Get your copy of "AI-Powered Agile: Revolutionizing Project Management with Artificial Intelligence" today!

Leveraging Generative AI in IT Project Management: A Practical Guide

"Leveraging Generative AI in IT Project Management: A Practical Guide" is an indispensable resource for IT project managers and professionals seeking to navigate the complexities of modern project landscapes with the innovative power of Generative AI (GenAI). This comprehensive guide begins with a foundational preface on GenAI's significance in IT project management and offers readers an instructive roadmap on utilizing the book to its full potential. This book covers all the essential grounds, from the fundamentals of GenAI technologies, key concepts, and their application in IT projects to the strategic integration of GenAI for project planning, documentation, and risk management.

Through detailed chapters, readers will learn how to set up their projects for success with GenAI, including choosing the right models, integrating AI into existing systems, and using GenAI for dynamic documentation and real-time project tracking. The book also delves into the softer aspects of project management, such as fostering an AI-ready culture, managing human-AI collaboration, and navigating the governance and ethical challenges AI technologies pose. With a focus on practical applications, each chapter is enriched with case studies, examples, and best practices for leveraging GenAI to enhance team collaboration, optimize resource allocation, and make strategic decisions.

Addressing future trends and innovations, the book prepares project managers for the evolving IT project management landscape, emphasizing the importance of sustainable and ethical AI development. The guide concludes with an epilogue that reflects on the paradigm shifts in project management and the enduring role of human ingenuity in an AI-driven world. Complemented by appendices offering a glossary of terms, resources for further learning, and a directory of software and tools, this guide is a must-have for anyone looking to leverage GenAI to drive project success in the digital age.

Marketing with AI: A Beginner's Guide to Free Tools and Techniques

Are you ready to unlock the transformative power of AI for your marketing – without breaking the bank?

In today's competitive landscape, AI isn't just for tech giants. This beginner-friendly guide empowers you to harness AI using free tools and transform your marketing strategy.

Inside, you'll discover:

Effortless Content Creation: Unleash AI to generate blog ideas, write compelling ad copy, and even design eye-catching visuals.

Brighter Social Media: Learn how AI analyzes your audience, spots trends, and helps you craft posts that get results.

Data-Driven Decisions: Ditch the guesswork! Use AI to understand your customers, personalize their experiences, and optimize your campaigns.

Step-By-Step Guidance: Simple tutorials and real-world examples make it easy to implement AI, even if you're a tech newbie.

This book is perfect for:

Small Business Owners: Grow your brand and reach new customers with AI-powered efficiency.

Marketers: Stay ahead of the curve and deliver campaigns that outperform the competition.

Anyone Curious About AI: Demystify the buzzwords and gain practical marketing skills that will future-proof your career.

Stop feeling overwhelmed by AI and start mastering it! Get your "Marketing with AI" copy today and transform your marketing success.

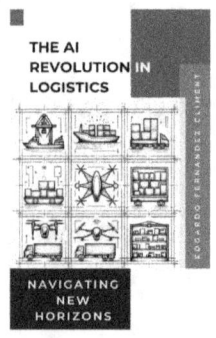

The AI Revolution in Logistics: Navigating New Horizons

Discover the transformative power of artificial intelligence (AI) in logistics with "The AI Revolution in Logistics: Navigating New Horizons." This comprehensive guide explores the latest advancements, use cases, and best practices for leveraging AI to optimize and revolutionize logistics operations.

As the logistics industry faces increasing complexity, customer expectations, and global competition, AI has emerged as a game-changing technology that can drive unprecedented efficiency, agility, and innovation. From demand forecasting and inventory optimization to autonomous vehicles and robotic warehouses, AI is reshaping every aspect of the logistics landscape.

In this book, you'll learn how to harness the power of AI to streamline your logistics processes, reduce costs, improve customer service, and gain a competitive edge. Key topics covered include:

The evolution of AI in logistics and its transformative potential

Key AI technologies and their applications in logistics, such as machine learning, natural language processing, computer vision, and robotics

Real-world case studies and success stories from industry leaders

Practical strategies for implementing AI in logistics, including data management, talent development, and change management

Ethical and responsible AI practices in logistics, including data privacy, algorithmic fairness, and human-machine collaboration

The future of AI-powered logistics, including emerging trends, challenges, and opportunities

Whether you're a logistics professional, supply chain executive, or technology enthusiast, "The AI Revolution in Logistics" provides the insights, tools, and guidance you need to navigate the AI-driven future of logistics. With expert insights, real-world examples, and actionable advice, this book is an essential resource for anyone looking to unlock the full potential of AI in logistics and stay ahead of the curve in this rapidly evolving industry.

Take advantage of the AI revolution in logistics. Order your copy of "The AI Revolution in Logistics: Navigating New Horizons" today and start your journey towards more innovative, faster, and more efficient logistics operations.

www.ingramcontent.com/pod-product-compliance
Lightning Source LLC
Chambersburg PA
CBHW052151220526
45471CB00004B/1621